AMERICAN EDUCATION

Its Men

Ideas

and

Institutions

Advisory Editor

Lawrence A. Cremin
Frederick A. P. Barnard Professor of Education
Teachers College, Columbia University

The Charity School Movement in Colonial Pennsylvania

Samuel Edwin Weber

ARNO PRESS & THE NEW YORK TIMES

New York * *1969*

Reprint edition 1969 by Arno Press, Inc.

*

Library of Congress Catalog Card No. 78-89251

*

Reprinted from a copy in the
Harvard College Library

*

Manufactured in the United States of America

Editorial Note

A MERICAN EDUCATION: *Its Men, Institutions and Ideas* presents selected works of thought and scholarship that have long been out of print or otherwise unavailable. Inevitably, such works will include particular ideas and doctrines that have been outmoded or superseded by more recent research. Nevertheless, all retain their place in the literature, having influenced educational thought and practice in their own time and having provided the basis for subsequent scholarship.

Lawrence A. Cremin
Teachers College

The Charity School Movement
in Colonial Pennsylvania

THE

CHARITY SCHOOL
MOVEMENT

IN

COLONIAL PENNSYLVANIA

THESIS

Presented to the Faculty of Philosophy of the
University of Pennsylvania

By SAMUEL EDWIN WEBER

In Partial Fulfilment of the Requirements for the
Degree of Doctor of Philosophy.

PRESS OF
GEORGE F. LASHER
PHILADELPHIA

PREFACE.

The history of the Charity School Movement has heretofore been related in connection with biographical sketches, in which the subject of the biography was more or less closely identified with the movement. The same may, with equal justice, be said of the discussions of the movement to be found in the various church histories. Such presentations of the subject must of necessity be incomplete. In many instances the facts are interpreted in the manner most favorable to the subject of the biography or to the church whose history is written. It is needless to say that no such interest enters into the present discussion of the movement. While the secondary sources have in no way been neglected, the aim has been to cite, as far as possible, the original sources only. In consequence, the references to secondary sources apply only to the original material to be found therein. The personal opinions set forth in the secondary sources have in nowise affected the conclusions arrived at in this treatise. The purpose of this dissertation is to present the material on the subject in a synthetic form and to arrive at the conclusions in the light of the facts presented.

The most helpful works on the subject are: "The Life of Rev. William Smith," by Horace Wemyss Smith; Harbaugh's "Life of Michael Schlatter;" "Hallesche Nachrichten," in two volumes, and Prof. W. J. Hinke's article, "Michael Schlatter," in the Pennsylvania German.

An effort has been made to avoid foot notes. Foot references to authorities are omitted altogether. The bibliography is arranged in alphabetical order, and each authority cited is numbered accordingly. For the purpose of ready verifications of the authorities cited, the number of the authority is first given, and immediately after, in case there is more than one reference to an author, the page of the particular citation is also given. After each source given in the bibliography appear the numbers of all the pages in a work to which reference has been made. The numbers enclosed in brackets refer to the page or pages of this treatise where the citation of the author occurs.

The writer feels under obligation to thank all those who have aided him in any way in this work. He owes a special obligation to Prof. W. J. Hinke for his suggestions of new original sources and for the use of such original sources as are in his possession.

For his constant assistance and encouragement, for the privilege of using his private library in which copies of almost all the Saur imprints are to be found, the writer takes this opportunity to thank Prof. Martin G. Brumbaugh, of this University.

SAMUEL EDWIN WEBER.

UNIVERSITY OF PENNSYLVANIA,
Philadelphia, Pa., April 14, 1905.

CONTENTS.

CHAPTER I. INTRODUCTION.

CHAPTER II. THE RELATION OF THE SOCIETY FOR
THE PROPAGATION OF CHRISTIAN
KNOWLEDGE AMONG THE GER-
MANS IN PENNSYLVANIA TO THE
CHARITY SCHOOLS.

CHAPTER III. THE ESTABLISHMENT OF THE CHAR-
ITY SCHOOL SYSTEM.

CHAPTER IV. FAILURE AND THE CAUSES OF FAIL-
URE.

INTRODUCTORY CHAPTER.

The influence of the Italian Renaissance manifested itself among the nations of Germanic origin in a deep religious feeling whose outcome was the Reformation (69:28ff). No sooner had the Lutheran and the Reformed faiths received equal recognition with the Catholic through the Treaty of Westphalia, in 1648, than the adherents of these faiths, still the subjects of persecution by the Roman Church, turned upon and persecuted those Protestants known as non-conformists who, as yet, had no ecclesiastical organizations. Of these there were a great many towards the close of the 17th century, including in their number Mennonites, Schwenkfelders, Pietists and Mystics (53:3f). By the beginning of the 18th century other sects came under the same ban. This persecution, instead of lessening, served only to increase the number of these dissenters. These unfortunate people thus became the victims of a double persecution—by Catholics and Protestants alike. The adherents of unorganized religious movements were at the mercy of one branch or other of the organized churches and were made to suffer for cherishing the same hope and striving to promulgate the same principles of truer, purer and holier living that animated their persecutors. William Penn visited these people in the Rhine Valley and in adjacent principalities in 1671, and again in 1677. Being himself persecuted on account of his religious tenets, he could preach to the inhabitants of Kriegsheim, Worms, Dreisburg, Duisburg, Crefeld, Emden and Westphalia the gospel of brotherly sympathy. Many warm friendships and religious attachments resulted from these visits. In 1681, when William Penn received from Charles II the territory, the major portion of what is now Pennsylvania and all of Delaware, translations of "An Account of the Province" were circulated through the Netherlands and the Rhine Valley in 1681 and 1683, respectively (53:14). Penn, naturally, founded his province as an asylum for the oppressed, a place where absolute religious and civil freedom was granted to all. An immediate invitation was extended to the Mennonites of Crefeld and vicinity to seek a refuge in Pennsylvania (31:29). In October, 1683, thirteen German Mennonite families landed in Philadelphia and at once,

under the leadership of Francis Daniel Pastorius, settled
Germantown (31:31). "This guarantee of religious and
civil freedom and equality, like the stroke of a magic wand,
called into lusty life the young giant of German immigration," says Professor Seidensticker (53:3). Subsequent
waves of German immigration were due largely to the
same cause. Dr. Jacobs (18:137f) sums up the facts of
the whole movement of German immigration when he says:
"Pennsylvania, we believe, became a favorite of German
emigrants because of the religious principles embodied in
its laws. These were, first, the clear recognition of Christianity as the basis of the government, and, secondly, the
toleration granted, within certain limits, for various forms
of Christianity. The fact that the German emigration pro-
ceeded in clearly marked waves, according to diverse denominations and sects, beginning with those most persecuted
in Europe, and thus proceeding to those where the religious
restraints in the mother country were more a matter of
annoyance than of persecution, supports this opinion."
From a letter* of Christopher Saur (47), dated the 15th
of March, 1755, it may safely be inferred that favorable
reports of the immigrants to their friends and acquaintances
in Europe constituted another strong cause of the German
influx.

There is no question that some Germans had settled in
Pennsylvania prior to the settlement of Germantown (10:
10), but these are in nowise connected with German immigration proper, having been absorbed by either Dutch,
Swedish or English civilizations (53:2).

From the time of the settlement of Germantown up to
1720 the German settlers were most largely composed of
Mennonites, Mystics and Dunkers (54:1ff). The Lutherans
and the Reformed had a few settlements, but the large body
of them came after that date (53:75). The Schwenkfelders
(20:35) and Moravians belong to a later wave of immigration; the former arriving in 1734, the latter in 1741 (35:81).

The earlier German settlements were confined to western
Montgomery, northern Chester, eastern Berks and the broad
plains of Lancaster and York counties. The counties of
Northampton, Lehigh, Lebanon, Dauphin and Adams were·
settled subsequently (52:233f).

We have no definite record of the number of Germans
that were in Pennsylvania prior to 1727. This number

---

* Original in possession of Dr. Martin G. Brumbaugh.

should include those who came into our borders as a result of the early Swedish settlements on the Delaware, the influxes from Manhattan and Long Island, N. Y. (10:105f), and from the Schoharie Valley, N. Y. (9:282), as well as those who came here directly from Europe. Two recent and authoritative investigators of the problem of early German immigration, Diffenderffer (10:102) and Kuhn (21:55), estimate the approximate number to be 20,000 before 1727.

In 1727 the Pennsylvania Assembly, becoming alarmed at the large army of Germans that were coming over, passed an act requiring all male ship passengers above the age of sixteen to take this oath of allegiance: "We Subscribers, Natives and late Inhabitants of the Palatinate upon the Rhine and Places adjacent, having transported ourselves and Families into this Province of Pensilvania, a Colony subject to the Crown of Great Britain, in Hopes and Expectation of finding a Retreat and peaceable Settlement therein, Do Solemnly promise and Engage, that We will be faithful and bear true Allegiance to his present MAJESTY KING GEORGE THE SECOND, and his Successors Kings of Great Britain, and will be faithful to the Proprietor of this Province; And that we will demean ourselves peaceably to all His said Majesties Subjects, and strictly observe and conform to the Laws of England and of this Province, to the utmost of our Power and best of our understanding" (62:283). The lists of oath-takers, together with the original ship registers make it possible to determine the annual increase of German settlers in Pennsylvania (36:49-419). Including the estimate of 20,-000, we have, up to the year 1755, about 80,000 German inhabitants in Pennsylvania (29:7-451). With the year 1749 these numbers reached their maximum. The records show that more than 7,000 came over in that year alone. The only previous year that will bear comparison with 1749 and the years immediately following, is 1738, when about 3,500 German immigrants arrived. A study of Rupp's "Thirty Thousand Names" discloses the fact that these immigrants came from various German localities. Prior to 1742 (36:49-152), all ships carrying immigrants included in their number passengers from the Palatinate. After that date they were characterized in Pennsylvania as "Foreigners or Strangers" from Swabia, Wurtemberg, Mannheim, Darmstadt, etc. Among these immigrants were many French Huguenots who had fled from France into various parts of Germany on account of religious persecu-

tion. Many of these had already adopted German names
and the German language (60:36f).

It is a singular fact in colonial history that Germans
settled in New Jersey, New York, Connecticut, Maine,
Virginia, Maryland, the Carolinas, Georgia and Pennsylvania, but nowhere did they settle in such large numbers
and, therefore, did not become such an influential factor in
molding the civilization, and determining state policies as
in Pennsylvania. By the middle of the 18th century the
German population exceeded more than one-third of the
State's total number of inhabitants (56:6). The reason
for their selection of Pennsylvania in preference to any
other colony has already been indicated, partially. Not
only did Penn's Frame of Government guarantee to these
Germans freedom of religious conscience and civil equality
such as no other province offered, but the soil and the
climate (22:14a) were better adapted to the needs of an
agricultural people, to which class the majority of these
colonists belonged (10:118). Gabriel Thomas, in 1697,
wrote this description of Pennsylvania: "The Air here is
very delicate, pleasant, and wholsom; the Heavens serene,
rarely overcast, bearing mighty resemblance to the better
part of France; after Rain they have commonly a very
clear Sky, the Climate is something Colder in the depth
of Winter, and Hotter in the height of Summer; (the cause
of which is its being a Main Land or Continent; the Days
also are two Hours longer in the shortest Day in Winter,
and shorter by two Hours in the longest Day of Summer)
than here in England, which makes the Fruit so good, and
the Earth so fertil" (63:9f). Those who in Germany had
learned such trades as glass-blowing, baking, or any form
of mechanical labor for which there was little demand in
Pennsylvania at this early date, were thus offered the best
alternative.

Incessant wars had made the great majority of these immigrants poor. Many had neither houses, lands, nor other
possessions. Others suffered the greatest want and pov-
erty (40:2). Those who left their fatherland in well-to-do
circumstances were reduced to beggary before reaching
Philadelphia. They became the prey of ship captains, ship
owners, sailors and passengers, who stole their money and
their goods (46). "Then with no more worldly possessions," says Professor McMaster, "than the clothes he had
on his back, and a few coins and a copy of the Heidelberg
Catechism he had in his pockets, he was at liberty to

earn the best living he could, save a few pounds, buy ten or
twenty acres of forest land, make a clearing and begin to
farm" (23:557). Here they lived in contentment. There
was no soldiery to meet them at every corner to compel
villainage. No exorbitant taxes were to be borne. A
mild government permitted them to enjoy the fruits of
their own labor without molestation. Their log cabins
were to them the equals of the stately palaces of many a
German nobleman (40:2). On the 9th of May, 1753,
Franklin, in a letter to Peter Collinson, compares the German laborer with the English: "When any of them (the
English) happen to come here, where labor is much better
paid than in England, their industry seems to diminish in
equal proportion. But it is not so with the German la-
borers; they retain their habitual industry and frugality
they bring with them, and, receiving higher wages, an ac-
cumulation arises that makes them all rich" (59:66).

William Smith (57:220), the first Provost of the University of Pennsylvania, placed the total population of the
State, in 1759, at 250,000. One-tenth of these were adherents of the Church of England, one-fifth were Quakers,
60,000 were English Anabaptists, English, Scotch and
Irish Presbyterians, Covenanters, and the remainder, with
the exception of a few English and Irish Catholics, were
Germans. These Germans at first, by tradition and by
reason of persecution in the fatherland, naturally abstained
from participating in governmental affairs and devoted
themselves to such peaceful occupations as the agricultural and textile industries (53.61). The contests lay between a war governor and the assembly composed most
largely of peace-loving Quakers. About 1750, when it
became a question as to whether the Quakers could
maintain control of the government in opposition to the
increasing war party, the Germans, warned by their
printer, Christopher Saur, of the danger of a repetition of
the miseries they suffered through wars in the fatherland,
went to the polls and threw the balance on the side of the
Quakers (56:29). This act of the Germans made them the
objects of reproach and misrepresentation by some of the
leaders of the advocates of State equipment for war.
Franklin (59:72) expressed fear for the prevailing language and government. Smith expressed himself as being
afraid that the Germans would unite with the French to
eject all the English inhabitants (56:31). He suggests
that the only way to prevent the occurrence of such mis-

fortunes is to educate the Germans to enable them to appreciate their true interests. "Give them faithful Protestant Ministers and Schoolmasters," says he, "to warn them against the horrors of Popish slavery; to teach them sound principles of government, to instruct their children in the English tongue, and the value of those privileges to which they are born among us" (56:34). Parliament is advised to pass a law: (1) denying the right of suffrage to the Germans for twenty years until they have a sufficient knowledge of the English language and the State constitution; (2) making all bonds, contracts, wills, and other legal writings void unless in the English tongue; (3) forbidding the printing and circulation of newspapers, almanacs, or any other periodical paper in a foreign language (56:41ff).

These charges were brought to the notice of the German inhabitants, and they resented the imputation of disloyalty to the proprietary government or to the British Crown. They remembered having taken the oath of allegiance when they arrived in Philadelphia. As early as 1706, we read that one hundred and fifty Germans, who had been twenty-two years in the country, were naturalized by the Provincial Council upon their petition (54:3). Again, in 1740, when an act of Parliament was passed for "naturalizing such Foreign Protestants as were settled or should settle in any of his Majesty's Colonies in America," those German Protestants who had lived in the province for a period of seven years, without having been absent from the province for a longer period than two months at any one time, and who produced certificates of having partaken of the Lord's Supper in some Protestant or Reformed congregation in the Province within three months, took and subscribed the oaths and became "natural born" subjects of Great Britain. This act was in force from 1740 to 1773 (30:347). In a letter to the Bishop of Exeter, dated April 23, 1748, Governor Thomas, who had been Governor of Pennsylvania from 1738 to 1746, bears the following testimony of the Palatines settled in Pennsylvania: "The Germans in that province are I believe three-fifths of the whole people, and by their Industry and Frugality have been the principal Instruments of raising it to its present flourishing condition beyond any of His Majesty's Colonys in North America. They all take the Oaths of Allegiance to the King of Great Britain in the presence of the Governor before they are permitted to make a settlement, and as far as I am capable of judging from nine years' residence in that Country, are like to continue as true to His Majesty and as useful to the British Nation as any of His Majesty's natural born Subjects" (32:256f).

The charge of secret conspiracy against the King and the State government cut these German Protestants to the quick. They maintained silence until November 20, 1754, when they issued an Address to Lieutenant-Governor Morris (30:686ff), assuring him of their continued loyalty to the Crown and to the State government. They declare that the charge is very hard "to a number of people against which no such Accusation can be aledged with justice, and against which, in general, not one single instance can be proved of any Disloyalty, much less of any Conspirace against our beloved King George and the Country we live in. * * * And being very well acquainted with the Sentiments of a considerable number of German Protestants, Inhabitants of this Province, who all unanimously agree to all what is above said, excepting a few ignorant unmannerly People lately come amongst us, it makes us the more free to lay the Case thus open before your Honour." The address is signed by about three hundred of their number, among whom appear the names of Michael Schlatter, Henry Muhlenburg, Peter Brunnholtz and Henry Antes. All of these men, as we shall find later on, were interested in the intellectual and religious welfare of their fellow countrymen. That the German was at least an average respectable citizen of the Commonwealth may be judged from the facts here adduced.

Let us see what intellectual qualifications for citizenship the large body of these immigrants had. Provost Smith (57:36), in a letter dated December 13, 1753, to the Society for the Propagation of the Gospel, represents the Germans as "utterly ignorant." Again, he (56:17) says, "one-half of the people are an uncultivated race of Germans, liable to be seduced by every enterprising Jesuit, having almost no Protestant Clergy among them to put them on their Guard, and warn them against Popery." Franklin (59:71), in the same year, says of them, "Those who come hither are generally the most stupid of their own nation." In the same letters just referred to, these eminent men describe the Germans in almost the same language. "They import many foreign books; and in Pennsylvania, have their Printing houses, their newspapers, and of late, their bonds and other legal writings, in their own language," says Smith (57:36). These letters seem to show that these men either were inconsistent in the presentation of facts or they confused ignorance with a lack of knowledge of the English language. The latter is probably the correct interpretation because Franklin (59:71f), before stating essentially the same facts as Smith, says, "Few of their children in the country know English." That they were not so utterly destitute of Protestant ministers, may be judged from Gottlieb Mittelberger's testimony. Having spent four years in the Province (1750-1754) as organist and schoolmaster, his countrymen in Pennsylvania implored him to write a true account of the condition of the Germans here so that their relatives and friends across the sea would not be deceived in coming to seek new homes for themselves. Among other things, he wrote, in 1755, "There are at present many good English, Swedish, Dutch and German preachers of the Lutheran and the Reformed churches in Pennsylvania" (24:60).

About 75 per cent. of these early immigrants, whose names appear on the ship-registers, were able to write their own name (19). Nearly all of those who signed their names to the Oath of Allegiance wrote in elegant German script. It is to be remembered that the record of names included all the males among the German immigrants above the age of sixteen. Taking the following years as typical, we find these percentages of illiteracy:

Year.	Per Cent.	Year.	Per Cent.
1727	24.46	1743	28.39
1728	26.00	1744	27.93
1729	29.85	1745	
1730	22.22	1746	18.36
1731	22.46	1747	18.57
1732	23.97	1748	17.56
1733	23.55	1749	23.25
1734	16.78	1750	28.03
1735	24.29	1751	22.08
1736	14.33	1752	18.30
1737	20.47	1753	14.14
1738	33.83	1754	17.34
1739	42.06		
1740	31.94	Total	645.50
1741	32.68		
1742	22.66		

645.50 ÷ 27 = 23.9 per cent.

Taking into consideration (1) that Germany had been the battleground of contending armies for more than a century, (2) the prevailing illiteracy in Europe at the time and (3) the additional fact that the Protestant Reformation laid emphasis on the ability to read rather than to write, the percentage of illiteracy is remarkably low. To the Protestant the Bible was the rule of faith for each individual. Ability to read the Scriptures, therefore, became an indispensable requisite. The only provisions for education to be found in Penn's Frame of Government (28:6) were, "That the governor and Provincial Council shall erect and order all public schools, and encourage and reward the authors of useful sciences and laudable inventions in the said province." . . . That there be "a committee of manners, education and arts, that all wicked and scandalous living may be prevented, and that youth may be successfully trained up in virtue and useful knowledge and arts." But since Penn gave to all classes of religion equal freedom they were permitted to teach their children in the manner they thought best. Education was thus vested in the hands of the Church and the religious motive predominated in the educational activity in Pennsylvania throughout the eighteenth century. The German was no exception to the rule. Prior to 1739 there were few German books published in the colony. As a consequence, books had to be imported (22:24a). The demand for books was great (57:36). Those most sought for were the Bible, the Catechism, the Testament, the Prayer Book and the Hymn Book (8:182). These were furnished by religious societies in Germany and Holland. Societies in Switzerland, Holland and Germany supplied those of the Reformed (13:160) faith; the Institution at Halle, the Lutherans (22:24a); the Dunkers in Germany raised by subscription a sum of money to purchase religious books and disperse them among their poor friends in Pennsylvania. Other denominations were equally solicitous. The effort of the Dunkers is of special merit because of the fact that a part of the funds raised was to be expended for a printing-press to be sent to Pennsylvania for the purpose of publishing religious books, a certain number of which were to be distributed among the poor Germans gratuitously (64:271). The history of this printing-press will be noticed later on.

Among the earlier immigrants there were ministers of the Gospel and some schoolmasters (38:7). Many schoolmasters who were dissatisfied with their condition in Germany came to Pennsylvania in the hope of improving their

lot. In the fall of 1749 as many as twelve arrived (22:432a).
Some of these came along with groups belonging to a particular religious denomination, their function being to instruct young and old for the success of the Gospel (37:440).
It was a common occurrence where people lived in thickly
settled communities to find in the schools as many as five
different religious faiths. Where a teacher used common
sense, he taught the children to read in such books as they
brought with them (41:25). Wherever such teacher had
opportunity to impart religious truths, applicable to all,
sensible patrons took no offense. It was frequently the
case where a community could not afford to support both
a schoolmaster and a minister, that the duties of both were
vested in one person (12:10). In many instances the
schoolmaster preceded the minister and prepared the way
for him. The Lutheran churches in Germany and the
Reformed churches of Switzerland and Holland had been
accustomed to engage a minister and a teacher (37:440f).
Each congregation was a religious unit in which the instruction was carried on by these two functionaries. Both
received a stated salary and were provided with a home
and a place of instruction. When these denominations
established churches in Pennsylvania they carried on the
same plan, so far as their funds would warrant it. Wherever there was a church, it was the practice to plant a
school. This was under the immediate supervision of the
minister and proved a valuable auxiliary to the church
(61:59f). It was a parochial system, *i. e.*, secular and religious instruction were not yet divorced. In the report
of May 21st, 1744, in the "Hallesche Nachrichten," Messrs.
Schaum and Kurtz (22:88a) are recognized as catechists
and schoolteachers for the Lutheran congregations in
Philadelphia, New Hanover, Providence and Germantown.
They were to teach the youth's of the different congregations reading, writing, arithmetic and other common
school studies, but "especially the Christian faith in harmony with the Holy Scriptures and the Lutheran Catechism, etc." Upon the request of the minister in charge
they were at stated times to preach and give catechetical
instruction and perform all those duties faithfully and diligently which otherwise devolve on a catechist and school-
teacher. Some of the other duties were: to lead the singing, play the organ and officiate at funerals in the absence
of the minister (68:140f).
The educational facilities for the Germans in Pennsyl-

vania prior to 1752 are clearly described in Saur's (41:24f) Almanac for that year, in a conversation between a settler who had arrived in Pennsylvania the previous year and an old inhabitant, who is presumably Saur himself:

"New-Comer. A matter that is of very great importance to me is, that, in Germany, one is able to send his children to school to have them instructed in reading and writing. Here it is well nigh impossible to get such instruction; especially, where people live so far apart. O, how fortunate are they who have access to a good teacher by whom the children are well taught and trained!

"Inhabitant. It is true. On that account many children living on our frontiers grow up like trees. But since the conditions are such that few people live in cities and villages as they do in Germany, it is natural that one meets with certain inconveniences. Where is there a place in this world where one does not meet with some objectionable features during his natural life?

"New-Comer. But this is an exceptional want, for if children are thus brought up in ignorance it is an injury to their soul's welfare,—an eternal injury.

"Inhabitant. That is true, but how few good schoolmasters there are! I myself have had many and known many, but few good ones have I seen. Yet, I remember two, in my life-time, who had many good qualities. The one spent most of his time in secret prayer and heartfelt sighing that God might direct and keep the hearts and minds of his pupils. He taught them their letters faithfully. He observed also their natural dispositions. If he found the child vain, then he would praise it so that it learned its lessons fairly well. He would promise that it should yet lead the class, but he asked God to take the devil's haughtiness out of the child's heart, to convert it and give it the lowly spirit of Jesus. After it had reached the head of the class he would tell it alone and in private that haughtiness came from the Devil, but humility was a quality of Christ's spirit for which the child should frequently and heartily join him in prayer to God. Thus he kept such children in his love. To those who were miserly he frequently gave a penny when they studied diligently and if they admired their gift he would tell them that money was the root of all evil, pointing out examples to them. He described for them deceptive riches and the subsequent disappointment if man is not rich in godly things. To the voluptuous and

"Leckermaüler"* he sometimes gave little lumps of sugar, when they learned well, but he also told them that luxuriousness was a sin, that those who belonged to Christ crucified the flesh with its lusts and evil desires. He impressed them so earnestly with these maxims that almost all the pupils loved him. If any failed in the performance of duty, he would say: 'I no longer love you.' Then they wept until he comforted them. The ill-intentioned, who were not affected by the promise of a penny or a cooky, he threatened with whipping. These then studied out of fear. With some he had to use the rod, but in each case he endeavored, first of all, to win their favor and thus secure obedience through love that they might not only learn their letters but that they might be able to seek, find and know Jesus himself.

"I remember still another one who, out of the love of God, loved his pupils as if they all were his own children. They, in turn, loved him dearly. Whenever he was obliged to reprove the children for ill-behavior, he did so with grievous words coming from his wounded heart, so that he frequently softened their hearts; and when they were about to cry, tears crept into his eyes. He studied out many plans so that he might not need to resort to the rod. On going to and from school the children went quietly and orderly without stopping to play, throw stones, loiter and quarrel. The children of the poor he taught as willingly without pay as he taught others for pay. Those who learned to write, he induced to correspond with one another. The pupils were required to show him the letters, and he pointed out for them the places where improvements should be made. He also told them that this was no ordinary matter. For those who could not compose a letter, he set copies so that they might apply their' minds to good thoughts for the improvement of their souls. He regarded it indifferently whether he received the tuition fees or not, and did not treasure up for himself anything but a good name and a good conscience.

"New-Comer. Such schoolmasters are few in number, and here in the woods one must be satisfied if only they teach the children to read and write; and it is very deplorable that, during the winter in severe weather, young and tender children cannot well be sent to schools a great distance from home. In the summer time one needs the

---

* Dainty-mouthed.

children at home to work, and here in the woods the schools are closed during the summer. I have often thought that this was a great need in this land, and I know of no remedy to suggest." The schoolmasters described by Saur have never been identified, but we have probable data that the former was the pious schoolmaster, Ludwig Haecker, who taught the children of the Dunkers in the house of Christopher Saur on each Sabbath afternoon. Shortly after his arrival in Ephrata, in 1739, he was appointed teacher of the common school. "After being a short time employed in this responsible position, he likewise opened a school in the afternoon of the Sabbath; aided by some of his brethren, imparted instruction to the poorer class of children, who were kept from regular school by employments in which their necessities obliged them to be engaged during the week, as well as to give religious instruction to those of better circumstances" (37:294). This Sunday-school was established about the year 1740. Haecker deserves the credit not only of being an ideal pioneer schoolmaster, but the movement of establishing Sabbath-schools which he inaugurated antedates by forty years a similar movement begun by Robert Raikes in Gloucester, England.

That the other schoolmaster whom Saur describes is Christopher Dock (31:91ff), who opened a school on the Skippack for the Mennonites as early as 1718, is evident from several well determined facts.\ Christopher Dock was the teacher of Christopher Saur, Jr., who was one of his great admirers, and through whose solicitation Dock wrote his Schul-ordnung in 1750, the first book written and published in America on School Management. Dock continued his work as a schoolmaster until 1728, and then he went to farming for another period of ten years. In 1738 he resumed his former occupation, opening schools in Skippack and Salford, teaching three days in each alternately each week. In his Schul-ordnung he describes his method of teaching letter-writing as follows (11:14f): "What now concerns the exchange of letters, it is to be remembered that I have for the past twelve years conducted two schools (which fact has been mentioned before), and also for four summers (namely, during the three months of vacation which I enjoyed on account of harvest) I kept school in Germantown. The pupils in Skippack, when I returned again to the school in Salford, gave me letters to take with me. On my return the pupils in Salford did likewise. The matter was so arranged that the correspondents were of equal advancement. If, in the course of time, one of the correspondents excelled the other, then he would write to one whom he hoped to equal. The superscription was only this: My friendly greeting to N. N. The contents of the letter were a short rhyme or a selection from the Bible, to which was added something concerning their school exercises, what they had for a motto during the week, and where it was written and the like." This book is of great value. It gives us a true picture of a German school in Colonial Pennsylvania. It describes in detail how the children should be received into school, how they were taught to spell, cipher, read and write, and how they were disciplined. His method of discipline is of special interest. He says on this point: "Experience in keeping school shows that a child, which is timid, if it is punished severely either with words or with the rod, is thereby more injured than benefited. If such a child is to be improved it must be by other means. In the same way a child that is stupid is more injured by blows than improved. A child which at home is treated with blows and is accustomed to them will not at school be made right by blows, but still worse" (11:25). Dock was in advance of his day when the rod was practically the only means to secure proper behavior. He studied the individual and adapted the punishment to the child's temperament and disposition. As was the custom among most schoolmasters in Colonial Pennsylvania, Dock emphasized religious instruction. The pupils were required to familiarize themselves with the Bible. In addition to a study of the Bible, he (51:15b) himself wrote hymns to be sung by the pupils in their devotional exercises (14:223).

The press has always been a powerful educational force among any people who are privileged to enjoy its influence. In 1753, Franklin (59:71) states, that "of the six printing-houses in the province, two are entirely German, two half German half English, and but two entirely English." From this statement by one who was a printer himself by profession, we may properly infer that the German population was on a par with their English neighbors, in so far as this means of disseminating knowledge was concerned. Among these presses that of Christopher Saur, in Germantown, was the most productive, and the most influential among the Germans. As early as 1738 there emanated from this press a German almanac and a German newspaper in 1739, both of which reached so large a circulation that they were said to have been "universally read" by the Germans (56:28). Prior to 1754 more than two hundred different publications were issued from the various German printing-presses (55:6-42). Most of the books printed were of a religious order. In 1743 Christopher Saur printed the first German Bible in America, thirty-nine years before the first English Bible was printed in America by Robert Aitken (70:28 and 56).

Notwithstanding the fact that these educational facilities were available to the Germans, secular instruction and religious instruction alike were inadequate in quality and quantity to result in an extensive culture. It is true that the Moravians, in 1743, under the personal direction of Count Zinzendorf, tried to assist their countrymen by opening here and there both day-schools and boarding-schools, but prior to 1754, there was no organized concerted effort on the part of the State officials to undertake a general system of education for the improvement of the intellectual, moral and religious condition of these Germans. The Moravians had established "union" schools at Muddy Creek, Lancaster, Oley, Mill Creek, Warwich, Heidelberg, Maguntsche, Walbach and Germantown, but, by 1754, they had all been given up, and thereafter the Moravians confined their educational efforts to the children of their own people (35:201ff).

Such, in brief, was the condition of the Germans in 1750. In many instances they lived too far apart to form themselves into congregations to receive religious instruction. "As it is with the schools, so it is also with the churches in the rural districts, because churches and school-houses are usually built around at such places only, where most neighbors and church members live," says Mittelberger (24:59ff). Even if they were able to form themselves into congregations they, frequently, had neither pastor nor teacher to instruct them (16:203ff). Some of those who assumed the offices of ministers and teachers were wholly unfit, intellectually and morally. The schoolmasters, in most places, were not able to support themselves on their income and were, in consequence, forced to earn their bread by manual labor. Many families were too poor to buy even bibles and catechisms for themselves and children (16:208). Muhlenberg (22:16a) asserts that youths of eighteen, nineteen and twenty years of age came to him for instruction. They had no knowledge whatever of reading and writing. They were equally wanting in a knowledge of God. Israel Acrelius (2:351), bishop of the Swedish churches in America, in 1758, says: "In almost every ridge is a schoolhouse." Again, he says: "None, whether boys or girls, are now growing up who cannot read English, write and cipher" (2:352). From what his contemporaries say, we may properly conclude that the report is exaggerated. Messrs. Kurtz and Schaum (22:73a), who taught schools in New Hanover and Philadelphia, respectively, taught young and old. The latter were not ashamed to sit with the children to learn their letters. In his diary of 1745 (22:418a) Muhleberg bewails the lack of Christian schools. He says: "In our parishes we have, up to this time, not been able to erect schools. Would that we might have in our communities and parishes but ten or twenty of the many hundred Charity Schools of England, where the children might be taught—if only for a short period during the year—it would aid us greatly."

The schools which were established in the province before 1750 were not able to accommodate the pupils who applied for admission. The buildings were too small and funds were not forthcoming to build larger ones (22:483a). The old teachers, who had come into the province with the earlier immigrants, were dying off, and there was no adequate provision made in the province to furnish substitutes (22:485a). Each succeeding year brought thousands of additional immigrants. The question in the minds of far-seeing statesmen was, "What step shall be taken to educate this increment to the population and make of them good citizens?" The answer to the question was to be found in "The Charitable Scheme to Educate the Poor Germans." What was the nature of this movement?

CHAPTER II.

The beginning of this movement starts with the labors of Rev. Michael Schlatter, who came to Pennsylvania, in 1746, under the direction of the Reformed Synod of Amsterdam (16:236). He was sent out as "church visitor" (65:6), whose duty it was to visit the Reformed congregations in America "in order to investigate whether the ministers and schoolmasters faithfully administer their offices, remain in the purity of doctrine and maintain the established order, etc." As most of the Reformed people that came to America had settled in Pennsylvania, the greater part of Schlatter's time was spent here. After five years of incessant labor he returned to Holland and reported the conditions as he had found them (16:198).

In his "Appeal to the Synod in Holland," dated June 25, 1751, he (16:213) pleads for the relief of his people: "My intercession is not for a handful of people, for one or another poor family, for a little flock that has fled from popery, but for more than 30,000 of the Reformed household of faith, living in the land of their pilgrimage, in a land that is large and wide spread, yea, fully twice as large as the United Netherlands. They are not concerned for gifts of love to be applied to the support of their lives and their temporal existence,—even though in this the want with many is great enough,—but such as shall be applied in the best possible manner, to procure means for the preservation of their immortal spirits, and those of their tender pledges, their children. If this help is not extended, and hearts and hands are closed against them, they and their children destitute of the means of grace, without the counsel of those who instruct, direct, exhort, edify and comfort them, they must in time sink into pagan blindness and fearful ruin. But should they be supported by your gifts of love, and provided with faithful teachers and pastors, they will, under God's effectual blessing, be brought to a sanctifying knowledge, and to the service and praise of the blessed God." Again, he says: "What makes the condition of these congregations the more deplorable and worthy of our sympathy, is that most of them are not even provided with a good schoolmaster. Few, even of such as are found qualified, can be prevailed upon to labor in this work, because the poor people are not able to contribute enough to enable a schoolmaster, who devotes his whole time to his calling, to support himself and family, even with the greatest care and economy. Thus, it is easy to see that children, deprived of all instruction, and having only a corrupt nature for their guide, must grow up as wild shoots —yea, I will leave any, who heartily and in silence meditate on this matter, and who know the true value of immortal souls, to judge whether in this way, even such as are called Christians and bear the name of Reformed, are not in danger of falling back and being corrupted into a new heathenism, and thus become like the original pagan aborigines of the country, if not even worse" (16:205).

The immediate effect of the appeal, after the case had been presented to the States of Holland and West Friesland (67:4), was the granting by those States of 2,000 guilders per annum for five years from that date, the same "to be applied towards the instruction of the said Germans, and their children in Pennsylvania." These funds were raised through the influence of the Prince of Orange, William IV. Additional sums of money were collected by the Synodical Deputies of Holland and the Classis of Amsterdam, making a total of nearly 45,000 florins. Professor Hinke's transcripts of the official reports of the Classis and Synods in Holland (65:13f) show that Reverend Muhlenberg's statement that 12,000 pounds (22:57b) had been collected in Holland was considerably exaggerated. In response to Schlatter's (16:248) plea for ministers and schoolmasters the Synods of Holland sent back with him six ministers "for carrying on the work of the Gospell" (6:106a).

David Thomson, a pastor of one of the English Reformed churches in Amsterdam, became greatly interested in the Pennsylvania German (67:4). In March, 1752, he left Holland to visit his countrymen in England and Scotland, in order to solicit aid from the churches in those countries for furthering the cause he had taken up. On May 22, 1752, Thomson's petition was taken up by the General Assembly of the Church of Scotland (6:104a). The three letters he offered to the Assembly were his credentials: (1) from the six deputies of the Provincial Synod of Holland, (2) from the Presbytery of Amsterdam, (3) from the Consistory of the English church there, "all setting forth and enforcing the purpose of his petition and commissioning him to agent the same" (6:107a). The Church of Scotland opened an immediate correspondence with the Protestant churches in Holland for the purpose of advancing, as they say (4:294), "the glory of our common Lord, and to promote and propagate the pure Reformed religion." In response to the petition the Assembly, "sensibly affected with the distressed state of their Protestant brethren in the British colonies" (6:107a), ordered a collection to be made at the church doors of all the parishes in Scotland on the last Sunday of the following November. This recommendation was ordered to be read from the pulpits of all the churches in Scotland the Sunday preceding the day named for the collection. The money collected (67:5) amounted to "upwards of twelve hundred pounds sterling" (£1,140 9s. 11d.) (6:312). The relation between the General Assembly and "The Society for the Propagation of Christian Knowledge among the Germans in Pennsylvania," may best be seen from the minutes of the former: "On Monday, June 4, 1753, Professor Cuming, the last Moderator, produced a letter from the Rev. Mr. Chandler at London, dated the 27th of February, bearing, that he, and several other gentlemen in London, had formed themselves into a society, to act as trustees for the Protestants in Pennsylvania; that they propose to maintain a stated correspondence with the Church of Scotland, with that in Holland, with several in Germany, and with the emigrants in Pennsylvania, that all moneys may be transmitted to them by a general agreement; that, in his judgment, all the collections made in Great Britain should center in the hands of the trustees there, who are to settle a correspondence in Pennsylvania, for the more proper distribution and application thereof; that six new ministers had already settled among the Protestants in Pennsylvania, and that six more are immediately wanted. After reading the letter, Professor Cuming represented, that as he had no opportunity of laying it before the commission, he had written a letter to Mr. Chandler, bearing, that as the Protestants in Pennsylvania are subjects of Gt. Britain, it would be necessary in order to make them more so by their learning the British language, to employ there some English school-masters for instructing their youth. And he now produced a letter from Mr.

Chandler, dated the 19th of May last, approving of the aforesaid proposal, which, he says, makes a principal article of a memorial presented to his Majesty; and further, expressing the intention of the said society to keep a constant correspondence with the church of Scotland by such persons as the Assembly shall appoint. The Assembly appointed all the money collected in Scotland for the Protestants in Pennsylvania, to be remitted to the aforesaid society at London, and nominated all the ministers of the Presbytery of Edinburgh, the Earl of Dumfries, the Lord Justice Clerk, Provost Drummond, and several other gentlemen, of whom four to be a quorum, a committee to correspond with them" (5:25f).

The Society to which Chandler refers consisted of fifteen of the most prominent men in England (57:41). They were the Right Hon. Earl of Shaftesbury, President; Right Hon. Lord Willoughby, of Parham; Right Hon. Sir Luke Schaub, Bart.; Right Hon. Sir Josiah VanNeck, Bart.; Thomas Chitty, Esq., Thomas Fluddyer, Esq., Aldermen of the City of London; Benjamin Amory, LL.D., James Vernon, Esq., John Bance, Esq., Robert Ferguson, Esq., Nathaniel Paice, Rev. Dr. Birch, Rev. Mr. Caspar Weitstein Rev. David Thomson, minister at Amsterdam, and the Rev. Samuel Chandler, Secretary.

On the 1st of December, 1753, Provost Smith (57:29) landed in London, and on December 13th he wrote a letter to the Society for the Propagation of the Gospel, in which he says, "My Lords and Gentlemen: For many years past incredible numbers of poor Protestants have flocked from divers parts of Germany and Switzerland to our Colony, particularly to Pennsylvania. Their melancholy situation, thro' want of instructors and their utter inability to maintain them, with the distressing prospect of approaching darkness and idolatry among them, have been represented to their fellow-protestants in Europe in the most moving terms."

A comparison of this paragraph with the first part of the Memorial (3:66) which was presented to the King by the Society, with the petition which Thomson presented to the General Assembly of the Church of Scotland, and with Schlatter's Appeal to the Fathers in Holland, reveals a striking resemblance in thought and language, and seems to indicate that Smith was familiar with the phrasing and tenor of thought in Schlatter's appeal and Thomson's petition.

Again, he says (57:30f), "Indeed it is deeply affecting to hear that this vast branch of the Protestant Church is in danger either of sinking into barbarian ignorance, or of being seduced at last from that religion for which they and their fathers have suffered so much. And should ever this be their misfortune, their Liberty itself, with all their expected use of these nations will be entirely lost. Besides this, their having no opportunity of acquiring our language, and their living in a separate body, without any probability of their incorporating with us, are most alarming considerations.

"In these circumstances, the scheme you have engaged in, to send instructors among these people, is of the greatest importance. The influence of a faithful clergy to form the social temper, to keep up a sense of religion, and guide such a people in their duty is obvious. Nor is the institution of schools for the education of their children a point of less, but perhaps still greater, importance. * * * * * * *

"By a common Education of English and German Youth at the same Schools, acquaintances and connexions will be form'd, and deeply impressed upon them in their cheerful and open moments. The English language and a conformity of manners will be acquired, and they may be taught to feel the meaning and exult in the enjoyment of liberty, a home and social endearments. And when once these sacred names are understood and felt at the heart;— when once a few intermarriages are made between the chief families of the different nations in each country, which will naturally follow from school acquaintances, and the acquisition of a common language, no arts of our enemies will be able to divide them in their affection; and all the narrow distinctions of extraction, etc., will be forgot—forever forgot—in higher interests."

In the paragraphs just quoted it becomes evident immediately that the religious motive for educating the German which Schlatter* exalted in his Appeal to the Fathers in Holland has become secondary to political motives which were to guide the efforts of the newly-established society. From the time of Professor Cuming's† suggestion to Chandler that the Pennsylvania Germans would become better subjects of Great Britain by employing English schoolmasters to teach them the English language, the question of the assimilation of this German element with

---

*See pp. 23f.   †See p. 25.

English civilization seems to have been uppermost in the minds of English statesmen. Schlatter did not question the loyalty of his countrymen to the Crown or to the proprietary government; in fact, we have seen on a previous page* that his name headed the list of signers of the petition addressed to Governor Morris. Smith (57:26ff), on the other hand, with the meager experience of five months with the Pennsylvania Germans was apprehensive of their loyalty. On the basis of this actual experience with them, and the reports he may have chanced to read of them in England, he put himself in touch with the Society in London for the Propagation of the Gospel. It is to be remembered that just at this time, the early 50's, the Germans began to take part in governmental affairs, throwing their influence to the Quaker as opposed to the proprietary government. The subsequent charge by Smith that the Germans were liable to join the French, the bitter enemies of the English, served as an additional reason for the Royal family and the Proprietaries of the Province to subscribe liberally to this movement.

The first reason for educating the German would be to make him independent in thought and action so that the Quakers could no longer use him as a tool to carry elections. Again, if the Germans were to unite with the French, England, in the event of a war with France, would be likely to lose her most prosperous colony. The former constituted a strong argument for the Proprietaries to aid the Charity School movement, and the latter would appeal even more strongly to the British Royalty so as to insure their support.

It is quite evident that the religious and political motives were not the only ones which determined Provost Smith's course of action. The 25th of May, 1753, he had been engaged temporarily, to teach "Natural Philosophy, Logic, etc.," in the College of the City of Philadelphia (57:26). Here was an opportunity for him to build up a great school, but he could not hope to draw students from the Quakers (68:43-57), for they had their own schools and were not on good terms with the proprietary government of which Smith (56:17f) was an ardent supporter, nor could he hope to gather students from the Presbyterian and kindred denominations, for they patronized the institutions which grew out of the Log College (27:66), and the followers of the Church of England (57:220) were but a small part of the State's total population, the other source

---

*See p. 13.
*See p. 13.

of patronage of the institution of which he was about to take hold. What was to be done? The answer was to be found in his ability to reach the German population in the State. This could only be done through the establishment of the Charity Schools as proposed by the Society in London. The masters for these schools should not be imported, but they should be educated and trained in Pennsylvania. The only institution in the State where that was possible was in the College of the City of Philadelphia. What does Mr. Smith say on this point (57:35f)? "The Masters of such schools can only be found and educated in America. They must understand the English and high Dutch, with Mathematics, Geography, Drawing, History, Ethics, with the Constitutions and interests of the Colonies. Now, strangers can not be thus qualified. For tho' they understood both languages, we could not be sure of their principles; nor would they for several years know the Genius of the people, or Correspond with the general Scheme of Polity in the education of youth; nay, they might be sent from the Palatinate or Switzerland to counter work it, and defeat the desired Coalition, Clergymen, Schoolmasters, Physicians, etc., have a natural influence over the people in the Country, and the constant importation of strangers of these professions is impolitic. Such men should be educated under the eye of the public in the colonies where they are wanted; and thus we will not only be certain if their principles, but also have them complete masters both of the English and German languages.

"It is a happy circumstance, in Pennsylvania in particular, that there is a flourishing Seminary, where such men may be educated; and happier still that the honorable proprietary is to make a foundation for maintaining and educating constantly some promising children of poor Germans as a Supply of well-principled Schoolmasters, that must be acceptable among their friends."

The funds which were thus to be raised by the London Society would serve not only to promote the religious welfare of the German colonists in Pennsylvania, the interests of the proprietary and Royal governments, but it would, incidentally, also aid Provost Smith's new project directly. The motives which thus seem to have actuated him were perfectly justifiable. Whether the attitude of the German toward the provincial government was as he had represented it, and whether the underlying schemes worked out successfully, are questions which do not concern us here.

The Society (67:7) raised funds in England, (1) by the liberal subscriptions of its own members, (2) the King granted £1000 toward the movement and the Princess Dowager of Wales contributed £100, (3) the Proprietaries of the Province promised to give an annual sum "for promoting the most essential part of the Undertaking."* Muhlenberg (22:208b) states that "these gifts, which it is said, amounted to 20,000 pounds sterling, were, by order of His Majesty, placed in the hands of certain trustees, constituting 'A Society for Propagating the Knowledge of God among the Germans,' from the interests of which free schools are here to be established and sustained." Professor Hinke has recently found a letter in the archives of the Classis of Amsterdam which proves conclusively, whatever the exact amount collected may have been, that not only the interest, but the capital was expended by the society in carrying on its work. Reverend Samuel Chandler, the Secretary of the society, in a letter written to the Classis of Amsterdam in 1762, says: "We have been so liberal in our expenditures in behalf of the schools and teachers of the continent of America, that the capital which here in England as well as in Scotland had been collected, has altogether disappeared, and hence we can now only depend upon his royal bounty." (65:14.)

The money which was granted so liberally enabled the Society for the Propagation of the Gospel to begin to carry out their purposes under very auspicious circumstances.

* This fund was intended primarily for the training of teachers.

CHAPTER III.

As soon as Dr. Smith (57:34f) learned of the intention of the London Society to establish schools among the Germans in Pennsylvania he formulated an educational plan and submitted it to the Society in his letter of December 13th, 1753. The scheme as thus outlined became the basis for the society's future procedure, so that the credit of the entire system belongs to Dr. Smith. He furnished the brains for this educational movement, and it is to him we must look for its success or failure, his English associates contributing to its execution only in so far as they co-operated with him.

The plan as set forth in the letter referred to above contains the following important recommendations:

1. "With regard to the government of the Schools, it is of the greatest use, in smaller Societies, where it is practicable, to have all places of Education uniformly governed by one set of men, that so youth may be everywhere trained up in subordination to the public Sense. This trust can only be executed by men residing on the spot, and therefore six or seven principal Gentlemen in Pennsylvania may be appointed Trustees-general for providing foreign Protestants in that and other Colonies with Ministers and Schoolmasters;

2. "One or more of these Trustees, is once every year to visit all the Schools and examine the Scholars, giving a small premium to one or more boys, born of German Parents, who shall best deliver an oration in English, or read an English Author, nearest to the right pronunciation. Let another premium be given to that boy, whether English or German, who shall best answer to some questions concerning religious and civil duties, on the plan already sketched out. And now, what a glorious Sight it will be to behold the Proprietor, governor or other great men, in their summer Excursions into the country, entering the schools and performing their part of the visitation. This will be teaching indeed like those ancient Fathers of their Country, who deigned to superintend the execution of the

laws they made for the education of youth as the rising hope of the State;

3. "But further, as the success of all Schools depends on good discipline and keeping up emulation, these Trustees-general should substitute six deputy-trustees for every School, three of them being English and three Germans, for the sake of forming more connexions. These deputies should visit the schools and bestow premia, as above, on every month, transmitting an account of such visitations to the Trustees-general, and these last sending once or twice a year an account of the whole state of the Schools to the Society in London. This scheme cannot fail of helping up discipline and emulation."

In compliance with these recommendations the London Society, "desirous to apply the moneys they collect in the most effectual manner for his majesty's service, the benefit of the Colonies and the welfare of these poor people" (57:40f), appointed as Trustees-general: The Honorable James Hamilton, Esq., Lieutenant-Governor of Pennsylvania; William Allen, Esq., Chief Justice; Richard Peters, Esq., Secretary of Pennsylvania; Benjamin Franklin, Esq., Postmaster-General; Conrad Weiser, Esq., Interpreter, and the Rev. William Smith, Provost of the College of Philadelphia.

The Society appointed Rev. Michael Schlatter Superintendent of these schools under the direction of the Trustees-general, and at an annual salary of £100 sterling. They agreed to erect schools in Reading, York, Easton, Lancaster, Skippack and Hanover. The masters were to receive an annual salary not exceeding £20 (57:42). As to the German ministers who were to receive aid from the Society no definite action was taken, pending further information from the Trustees-general, whose intimate knowledge of conditions would enable them to suggest specifically where such aid was most needed.

When Dr. Smith (57:45) returned to Philadelphia, May 22d, 1754, he endeavored to call a meeting of the Trustees on May 30th, but as Messrs. Peters, Franklin and Weiser had gone to Albany as commissioners of Pennsylvania to consider the Indian Treaty, the first meeting of the Trustees had to be postponed until after the return of these gentlemen. On the 10th of August, 1754 (57:64), the Trustees-general met in Mt. Airy, at the house of William Allen, and resolved to erect schools at Reading, York, Easton, Lancaster, Hanover and Skippack. They also resolved:

"That, for the better government of these schools, a certain number of the most reputable persons residing near every particular school should be appointed deputy-trustees, to visit that school, superintend the execution of the scheme of education in it, and use their interests in the support of it.

"That six, eight or ten be appointed for every school, and that, to render the scheme more catholic and unexceptional, part of these trustees for each school shall be Calvinists, part Lutheran Germans and part Englishmen of any profession whatever."

The only difficult problem that presented itself thus far was the supply of proper schoolmasters. A temporary relief was found in drawing on the Academy of Philadelphia for those poor students who could talk English and German (an indispensable requisite for teachers in the Charity Schools). A continuous supply of such students, Dr. Smith (57:65f) informed the Trustees, could be furnished by the Academy of Philadelphia owing to the annual gift of £50 sterling by the Honorable Thomas Penn, at his disposal for such a purpose. Dr. Smith also informed the Trustees that he had found a promising young man, Samuel Magaw, who might be prepared at the Academy in six or eight months for a position in one of these schools. With that purpose in view he had prevailed upon the Reverend Peter Brunnholtz, the Lutheran pastor of St. Michael's Church in Philadelphia, "to board Mr. Magaw in his home, to watch over his morals, and assist him in making further progress in the German language, provided the trustees would admit him to the proprietaries' bounty." The trustees accepted the proposition, and inquired for more promising candidates who could be fitted to teach in the schools.

Thus far we can say, without any qualification, Dr. Smith's scheme succeeded without any serious obstruction. The movement was supported by those Germans who belonged to the Reformed Church, (1) by virtue of the co-operation between the "Fathers in Holland" with the London Society for the Propagation of the Gospel among the poor Germans in Pennsylvania, (2) by the additional fact, that the leader of the Reformed Church in Pennsylvania was the superintendent of these schools. The Lutheran (17:279) element was favorable to the new project on account of its "nearness" to the Church of England for whose interests Dr. Smith put forth every effort. Rev. Muhlenberg, as we have shown already, longed for some of the charity schools in England to teach the youth in Pennsylvania.* Besides these considerations, Muhlenberg longed for an institution where the clergy in the Lutheran Church might be educated (61:69). This could be accomplished in the best manner by co-operating with any movement in which the authorities of the College and Academy of Philadelphia were interested. With these ends in view, Muhlenberg lent his best efforts to encourage the establishment of schools. In consequence, Dr. Muhlenberg's congregations in New Hanover and New Providence were the first to petition the trustees, August 23d, 1754, for schools, offering their newly-built school houses for the use of the respective communities (57:80f). But the mistake of the whole movement was the disregard it showed to the Quietist Sects of the Province. These, according to Smith's table, numbered upwards of thirty-five thousand people (57:220). Among these were the Mennonites, Moravians, Dunkers, Schwenkfelders, Siebentagers, all of whom were opposed to the bearing of arms and the taking of oaths on account of their religious scruples. It is to be remembered that these were the people who fled from Germany on account of their suffering persecutions at the hands of those religious denominations which had church organizations. Memories of their former experiences still lingered with them, and on the first grounds for suspecting the movements of the organized churches in America they arose, and in their might strove valiantly against this movement, which they considered an encroachment on their religious liberty. Those Germans who belonged to the Reformed and Lutheran faiths needed only to be made aware that this movement of establishing English Charity Schools among them involved the integrity of their language and nationality, and they were ready to join hands with the Quietist Sects to check the progress of the movement, and ultimately destroy it. The voice which unified German sentiment and gave it such powerful expression was Christopher Saur, the German printer of Germantown, from whose press emanated most of the German literature that was to be found among the eighty or ninety thousand Germans in Pennsylvania.† Let us

---

*See p. 22.   †See p. 37.

see what made Saur and his press such potent factors in determining public opinion among the Germans.

The press, types and books which the Dunkers* in Germany sent to their brethren in Pennsylvania fell into the hands of Jacob Gans, of Germantown. On account of Gans' incapability to carry out the original purposes of the Brethren, the entire property was transferred to Christopher Saur, in 1738, who, says Thomas in his History of Printing (64:271), "immediately began business according to the benevolent intentions of those who were at the expense of the establishment. The German books sent over were distributed gratuitously among the poor. The press was set to work on religious tracts, and a proportion of them given away. Others were sold and produced a profit to the printer. In a short time Sower so managed the concern as to gain the approbation of his opposers." Saur was intensely interested in the moral, religious and intellectual welfare of his countrymen. Himself a man of a high religious and moral sense, with an intellectual training (7:345) second to that of few men in the Province, he set to work to give his countrymen, so far as lay in his power, the same opportunities which he had had.

In 1738 he published the first "High-German American Calendar." This almanac appeared annually for thirty-nine years, printed by the elder Saur up to 1758, and then by his son up to 1778. These almanacs were a constant guide to nearly all the German families settled in Pennsylvania and the other provinces. In them were found medical prescriptions, directions to the farmers as to the best time for planting and reaping, dissertations on such subjects as "Lives of Great Men," "Necessary Precautions in Business Transactions," "The Force of Habit," "War and Peace," "The Indian," "The Use and Abuse of Brandy," etc. In addition to these, there were definite instructions given to those who desired to read and write in the English and the German languages (45:24). Blank sheets were inserted in some of the almanacs to serve as account books for the German farmer. In 1739, appeared "The High-German Pennsylvania Gazette," a weekly newspaper, which continued up to 1778, and as early as November, 1753, the number of subscribers was 4,000 (42:3). This periodical was devoted to the publishing of foreign and domestic news, and continued to ap-

---

*See p. 15.

pear regularly, under various titles, up to 1778. In 1739, (55:11) also appeared the first book printed with German type, "Weyrauchs Hügel," a collection of hymns covering over eight hundred pages. In 1743 Saur printed his first edition of the German Bible, the first Bible printed in America in a foreign tongue, the only previous edition printed in America being Eliot's (70:9) Indian version of 1663. Saur (39:1) states in the preface to the edition of 1743, his reasons for issuing the Bible at that time: "The motives which led to the printing of this present Bible were principally these: First, it was observed that many poor Germans came to this country without bringing any Bible with them, and secondly, that many among those born and reared here, do not know how to procure one— the wealthy, we notice usually providing for themselves and family only." To bring the Bible within reach of all who desired it he sold it (to those who could afford to pay) for eighteen shillings bound, and fourteen shillings unbound, "but to the poor and neady," he said, "we have no price." (70:48.)

The Bible was a royal quarto of 1,248 pages, $7\frac{1}{2}$ x 10 inches, bound in bevelled boards, covered with strong leather, the covers being held together with clasps. The edition, Wright (70:40) says, consisted of 1,200 copies. When the elder Christopher Saur died, in 1758, his son, Christopher Saur, took up the work with the same spirit and earnestness his father had shown before him. In 1763, the younger Saur issued the second edition of the German Bible, in the preface of which he could say (50:1): "There appears now for the second time, on this American continent, the Holy Scriptures, called the Bible, publicly printed in the High German language; to the glory of the German nation, inasmuch as no other nationality can claim that the Bible has been printed in their language in this part of the world." The success which attended the issuing of this edition enabled Saur to offer gratis to the subscribers of his newspaper copies of a religious periodical called "A Spiritual Magazine" (51:410). This magazine was first printed in 1764, and appeared monthly until fifty numbers had appeared. From 1768 to 1770 the magazine was discontinued because of the fact that Saur had in preparation the third edition of the German Bible. He did not wish to raise the price of his Bible by purchasing more paper than he had on hand for the publishing of the same, and thus the magazine was discontinued until 1770, when he re-

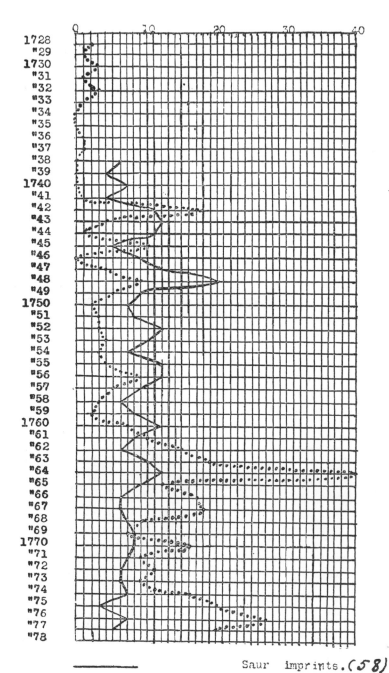

Saur imprints. *(58)*

........All other German imprints. *(55 : 6-100*

sumed its publication until fifteen numbers of the second part appeared. The contents of these numbers consisted of extracts of Scripture passages taken from the Old and the New Testaments, and extracts from non-sectarian religious writings to be found in the English language as well as in the German language (51:a3). Each number consisted of a half-sheet (16 pages). The first numbers consisted of translations of Archbishop William Law's "An Serious Call to a Devout and Holy Life." It ought to be evinced by these facts that neither of the Saurs was opposed to the education of the German, that they were not narrow in their views nor prejudiced to favor one class of Germans more than another. Christopher Saur, Sr., believed in a free public school system, and was a pioneer in prophesying a definite date when Pennsylvania should enjoy the same. The actual facts indicate that his prophesy set the date nine years too early, for our public school system was instituted in 1834 (68:313). In his almanac for 1754 (43:24), under the caption, "The Condition of the Germans in Pennsylvania in the Year 1825, if They so Desire," he says, "Then they (the Germans) will have a prosperous free-school to which all religious denominations will send their children. * * * * The German will be able to get legal advice from an honest fellow-brother who speaks both languages in their purity." There is ample evidence that Christopher Saur, Jr., appreciated the value of an education. The records of the Germantown Academy show that, in 1759 when the institution was founded, Christopher Saur was appointed a member of the first Committee on Subscription "to raise funds to erect the building" (66:8). He was one of the favorites on the Board of Trustees, being chosen twelve times to serve in that capacity. He was the first President of the Board of Trustees, and his name appears second on the "Committee on Subscription" (66:10). As a member of the latter, he was one of the most liberal contributors, giving "£50 from his father's estate and £20 in his own name" (66:13).

An examination of the graphic table of German publications in Pennsylvania, from 1728 to 1778, will show that the Germantown press was predominant throughout the period of the Charity School movement (1754-1764). It also shows that the publications of the two Saurs were the one unfailing source which supplied the Germans with literature of all kinds from the establishment of the Germantown press to the time of the Revolution. By virtue of this great supply of literature to the Germans Christopher Saur gained great power and influence among them. As a consequence, he became a great factor in determining the success or failure of any movement which might be projected to effect materially the welfare of the German. The "scheme" for establishing Charity Schools appealed to him as wrong because of its apparent political and religious motives, and he opposed it with all his might.

In Saur's Pennsylvanische Berichte of June 26, 1754 (57:48), he says: "We hear that ambition, etc., has made a provision in the Academy of Philadelphia for Germans who have no mind to get their living by honest labor, probably under pretext of raising lawyers, preachers and doctors, since so little honesty comes in from abroad. But as human weakness values things that come in from far, much more than what is daily in view; and, whereas, one has liberty in Pennsylvania to call a shilling a shilling, those that have got their learning from Empirics shall expect but little encouragement in this country, since 'a prophet himself has no honor in his own country.' "

In the same paper, on the 1st of September, of the same year, Saur (44:2f) attacks the movement directly: "In our number 159 we committed an error in saying that a High School was to be erected in Philadelphia for the benefit of the Germans, etc. But definite information is given that six English free schools are to be established in this State for the Germans in the cities of Philadelphia, Lancaster, York, Reading, Easton, etc. German ministers are urged to learn to preach in English so that the Germans may by degrees become one nation with the English, and be provided with English clergymen. These accounts further tell us that this was done out of fear that the multitude of Germans might make up or form themselves into one separate people or body, and in time of war go over to the French, and join with them to the hurt of the English nation.

"The new society in England deserves praise for being so liberal and so kind as to teach the Germans the English tongue gratis. But if Schlatter* has accused the Germans to such a degree, and represented them as if they were a nation of so roguish and mischievous a disposition, that in

---

* Saur is in error in preferring this charge against Schlatter, for Schlatter's name heads the list of those Germans who protested to Governor Morris against a similar charge of disloyalty. Smith and Franklin are responsible for these reports in England.

time of war they would probably join the French and villainously espouse their cause, he has certainly acted with great imprudence, to the disadvantage of the King as well as of himself. None, indeed, will permit themselves to think that many Germans could be so treacherous as he perhaps may think. The Irish, the Swedes and the Welsh keep their languages, yet for all that are not looked upon as a disloyal people. Oh, that pious school-masters in the English tongue might be given them, who could be to them a pattern of a true Christian life! Then still some hopes would be left, some good might proceed therefrom; for it is true piety only that makes men faithful towards God and their neighbor. The preacher Solomon says, Chap IX., v. 18, 'Wisdom is better than weapons of war; but one sinner destroyeth much good.' The wicked man may either preach English or German, yet it is no purpose or benefit, for no soul shall be mended thereby, nay, not himself."

The Society in London felt the influence of Saur and determined to counteract it by establishing a printing press in Philadelphia. They hoped to dispose the minds of the German population more kindly toward the designs of the Society by circulating among them German newspapers, almanacs, Bibles, catechisms, etc. (57:69). The Trustees-general purchased a press from Benjamin Franklin (57:96) for £109 8s. 4d. sterling at a special discount of £25, Franklin being one of their number and, consequently, interested in this educational work. The press was under the management of Anthony Armbruster from the time of its establishment, 1755 to 1759, when Armbruster failed in business and Peter Miller and Ludwig Weiss, conveyancers, gained control of the press, retaining Armbruster as compositor (55:52). Not only was the press bought and equipped with funds raised by the London Society (57:70), but the printer was offered a house, a few acres of land, £20 sterling per annum for teaching school, and additional wages for services as printer. The editor-ship of the newspaper was tendered to Reverend Henry Melchior Muhlenberg (55:45). Muhlenberg declined, but recommended another Lutheran minister for the place, Reverend Johann Friedrich Handschuh, who accepted the position. The paper, "Philadelphische Zeitung," edited by Handschuh, first appeared July 12, 1755, and was discontinued with the number dated December 31, 1757.

Dr. Smith's report of October 3, 1755, to Secretary Chandler gives one a general idea of the early history of this press (57:97):

"The German newspaper succeeded well; there being upwards of 400 subscribers, and more daily coming in. But it is so very low that it will do no more than clear itself, and that not until the year's end; so that there must be a considerable advance for paper and for the director of the Press. But after the first year all this may be saved, and we must ease you in the other articles; for the paper may do more good to the design than several schools, because the Director has express orders not to meddle with any of the disputes in this province, but to strive in every paper to say something to improve and better his countrymen and to confirm them in the Love and Knowledge of the Protestant Religion and civil Liberty. There are also 3,000 Dutch almanacs for 1756 printed, by which article we shall be gainers." The Society failed to realize the high hopes they had set on the future efficient service of this press. Their printer was continually in debt, and the restraints placed on the editor prevented him from writing any but the most conservative editorials. There was little life and originality in them to create enthusiasm among the Germans for the Charity School movement. The very thing it needed most of all was thus not forthcoming (57:88f).

On December 10, 1754, Dr. Smith, the Secretary of the Trustees-general, read before the trustees a pamphlet, entitled "A Brief History of the Rise and Progress of the Charitable Scheme, Carrying on by a Society of Noblemen and Gentlemen in London, for the Relief and Instruction of poor Germans, and their Descendants, settled in Pennsylvania," etc. Of these pamphlets, 2.300 were printed for distribution among the Germans and such English people as were interested in the solution of this religious and political problem. Dr. Smith first sets forth the two main objects of the London Society. These objects are (67:7f):

"I. To assist the People in the Encouragement of pious and industrious Protestant Ministers, that are, or shall be, regularly ordained and settled among the said Germans, or their Descendants, in America; beginning first in Pennsylvania, where the Want of Ministers is greatest, and proceeding to the neighboring British Colonies as they shall be enabled by an Increase of their Funds.

"II. To establish some Charitable Schools for the pious

Education of German Youth of all Denominations, as well as those English Youth that may reside among them, etc."

The stipulation that the children of English parents living in German settlements were to have the benefit of these schools makes the "scheme" more or less general in its application. The fact that the State officials were the trustees of the movement makes it our first State system of public education.

As to the method and purpose of establishing these schools, the course of study, the qualifications of teachers, etc., the pamphlet referred to on a previous page contains the following interesting items (67:10ff):

"First, it is intended that every School to be opened upon this Charity, shall be equally for the Benefit of Protestant Youth of all Denominations; and therefore the Education will be in such Things as are generally useful to advance Industry and true Godliness. The Youth will be instructed in both the English and German Languages; likewise in Writing, Keeping of common Accounts, Singing of Psalms, and the true Principles of the holy Protestant Religion, in the same Manner as the Fathers of these Germans were instructed, at the Schools in those Countries from which they came.

"Secondly, as it may be of great Service to Religion and Industry, to have some Schools for Girls also, we shall use our Endeavors with the honorable Society, to have some few Schoolmistresses encouraged, to teach Reading, and the Use of the Needle. And tho' this was no Part of the original Design, yet as the Society have nothing but the general Good of all at Heart, we doubt not they will extend their Benefaction for this charitable Purpose also.

"Thirdly, that all may be induced, in their early youth, to seek the Knowledge and Love of God, in that Manner which is most agreeable to their own Consciences, the Children of all Protestant Denominations, English and Dutch, shall be instructed in any Catechism of sound Doctrine, which is approved of and used by their own Parents and Ministers. All unreasonable Sort of Compulsion and Partiality is directly opposite to the Design and Spirit of the Charity, which is generously undertaken to promote useful Knowledge, true Religion, public Peace, and Christian Love, among all Ranks and Denominations.

"Fourthly, for the Use of the Schools, the several Catechisms that are now taught to Children among the Calvinists,

Lutherans, and other Protestant Denominations, will be printed in English and Dutch and distributed among the Poor, together with some Bibles and other good Books, at the Expense of the Society.

"Fifthly, in order that all Parents may be certain of having Justice done to their Children, the more immediate Care and Inspection of every School will be committed to a certain Number of sober and reputable Persons, living near the Place where every such School shall be fixed. These Persons will be denominated Assistant or Deputy-Trustees; and it will be their Business, monthly or quarterly to visit that particular School for which they are appointed, and see that both Master and Scholars do their Duty. It will also be their Business to send an Account of the State and Progress of the Schools, at every such Visitation, to us as Trustees-General. These Accounts we shall transmit from Philadelphia to the Society in London; and the Society will, from Time to Time, be enabled, by these Means, to lay the State of the whole Schools before the Public; and thus charitable and well disposed People, both in Great-Britain and Holland, seeing the good Use that has been made of their former Contributions, will be inclined to give still more and more for so glorious and benevolent an Undertaking.

"This Method cannot fail to be of great Advantage to the Schools, since these Deputy-Trustees, being part of the very People for whom the Work is undertaken, and having their own Children at the same Schools, they must have an Interest in the Reputation of them, and do all in their Power to advance good Education in them. Besides this, being always near at Hand, they can advise and encourage the Master, and help him over any Difficulties he may meet with.

"But Sixthly, as the keeping up a Spirit of Emulation among the youth is the Life of all Schools, therefore, that we may leave as little Room as possible for that Remissness, which sometimes hurts Charities of this Nature, we shall (as far as our Situation will permit) have a personal Regard to the Execution of the Whole. As the Assistant-Trustees may often want our Advice in removing Difficulties and making new Regulations, we shall so contrive it, that Mr. Schlatter shall be present with them at their Quarterly Meetings, to consult with them, and concert the proper Measures to be taken. Besides this we shall have one general Visitation of the whole Schools every Year; at which one or more of us shall endeavor to be present. On these Occasions, such Regulations shall be made whether any Parents think themselves injured, by an unjust Exclusion of their Children from an equal Benefit of the common Charity, or by the Partiality of the Master, or otherwise. At such Visitations Books will be given as Rewards and Encouragement, to the diligent and deserving Scholars. The Masters will likewise have proper Marks of Esteem shewn them in Proportion to their Fidelity, and Industry in the Discharge of their Office.

"Seventhly, with Regard to the Number of Schools to be opened, that will depend partly on the Encouragement given by the People themselves, and partly on the Increase of the Society's Funds. A considerable number of Places are proposed to fix Schools in, but none are yet absolutely determined upon, but New Hanover, New Providence, and Reading. These Places were first fixed upon, because the People of all Persuasions, Lutherans, Calvinists, and other Protestants, moved with a pious and fatherly Concern for the illiterate State of their helpless Children of all Denominations in these Parts, might be made the common object of the intended Charity. And for this benevolent Purpose, they did farther agree to offer School-houses, in which their Children might be instructed together, as dear Fellow-Christians, redeemed by the same common Lord and Savior, and travelling to the same heavenly Country, thro' this Valley of Tears, notwithstanding they may sometimes take Roads a little different in Points of smaller Moment.

"This striking Example of Unanimity and good Agreement among all Denominations, we hope, will be imitated by those who shall afterwards apply to us for fixing Schools among them; since it is only upon the aforesaid generous Plan for the common Benefit of all, that we find ourselves empowered to institute such Schools. But while the Petitions are agreeable to this our Plan, as now explained, they will not be overlooked, as long as the Funds continue. And if the Petitioners shall recommend Schoolmasters, as was the Case at New Hanover, New Providence, and Reading, such Schoolmasters, will have the Preference, provided they are Men of sufficient Probity and Knowledge, agreeable to all Parties, and acquainted with both the English and Dutch Languages, or willing to learn either of these Languages which they may not then be perfectly acquainted with.

"These are essential Qualifications; and unless the generous Society had made a Provision for teaching English as well as Dutch, it would not have answered their benevolent Design, which is to qualify the Germans for all the Advantages of native English Subjects. But this could not have been done, without giving them an Opportunity of learning English, by speaking of which they may expect to rise to Places of Profit and Honor in the Country. They will likewise be thereby enabled to buy or sell to the greater Advantage in our Markets; to understand their own Causes in Courts of Justice, where Pleadings are in English; to know what is doing in the Country round them; and, in a word, to judge and act entirely for themselves, without being obliged to take Things upon the Word of others, whose Interest it may be to deceive and mislead them."

The Trustees-general immediately began to carry out this plan. The Assistant-Trustees for the various places in which schools were to be established were, for the most part, personally known to Governor Hamilton, Secretary Peters and Indian Interpreter Conrad Weiser (57:71f).

For Lancaster.—Edward Shippen, Esq. (English), President; Mr. Adam Simon Kuhn, Mr. Otterbein, Mr. Sebastian Groff (Calvinist), Mr. Gera (Lutheran), Mr. James Wright, Mr. John Bar.

For New Providence and Skippack.—Mr. Abram Sahler, Dr. John Diemer (Calvinist), John Schrack, Nicolaus Küster (Lutheran), Henry Pawling, Esq., Mr. Robert White, John Coplin (English).

For Reading.—Mr. James Read, Prothonotary, Francis Parvin, Esq. (English Quaker), James Seely (English Presbyterian), Mr. Isaac Levan, Mr. Samuel High (Calvinist), Mr. Hans Martin Gerick, Mr. Jacob Levan (Lutheran), Mr. Sebastian Zimmerman.

For Easton.—Mr. Parsons, Mr. Lewis Gordon, Mr. John Chapman, Mr. John LeFevre, Mr. Peter Trexler.

For New Hanover, Frederick Township.—Andrew Kepner, Henry Krebo (Lutheran), Henry Antes, Esq., Mr. John Reifsnyder (Calvinist), John Potts, Esq., William Maugridge, Esq. (English).

For York no one was appointed, but Conrad Weiser was instructed to find, on his next journey to the frontiers, proper persons in York who were to receive the appointment of trustees. The original intention of the Trustees-general was to establish twenty-five schools among the

Germans in Pennsylvania. Eighteen (57:102) petitions were received for schools, but the records show that not more than twelve were ever established. This was due to lack of funds, an inadequate supply of teachers, and, in some cases, failure among the petitioners to agree on a location. The schools for girls were not considered as urgent and their establishment, with the exception of the school in New Providence where a few girls were taught reading and sewing by Mrs. Rabatan (57:93), was postponed indefinitely. All the schools established were boys' schools.

The Reformed and Lutheran congregations of Vincent Township petitioned the Trustees for a school, December 26th, 1754. The trustees granted the petition and appointed Louis Ache (57:89), schoolmaster at £20 per annum. For better preparation in English he was to be sent to the Academy of Philadelphia at the expense of the Proprietaries. The local trustees appointed were: Sebastian Wagner and Peter Stager (Calvinists), Michael Heilman and Conrad Shreiner (Lutherans), Samuel Hover and Richard Richardson (English).

At the same meeting a similar petition was received from Upper Salford Township, Montgomery County. Reverend Frederick Schultz, the Lutheran minister, was chosen to teach the school at £30 per annum.

The inhabitants of Lancaster (57:90f) petitioned the Trustees-general for a charity school in which the children of the poor were to be taught the English language, and as some of the parents desired to have their children instructed in Latin and Greek but had not the means to support a separate master for the purpose, they requested that a teacher be appointed who was "acquainted with these learned languages." To aid the Society in establishing such a special school, sixteen of the most substantial citizens of Lancaster, English and German, subscribed as follows:

		Per Annum.	
Edward Shippen, 2 scholars, though he has none to send	£6	0	0
Simon Kuhn, 2 scholars	6	0	0
George Gibson, 2 scholars	6	0	0
Michael Utt, 1 scholar	3	0	0
Emanuel Carpenter, 1 scholar	3	0	0
George Ross, 1 scholar	3	0	0
George Craig and James Wright, 1 scholar	3	0	0
Michael Gross, 1 scholar	3	0	0
Jacob Good, 1 scholar	3	0	0
William Sloon, no scholar	1	10	0

	Per Annum.		
Jacob Eichholtz, 1 scholar	3	0	0
John Jacob Loeser, no scholar	1	10	0
Bernard Hubley, 1 scholar	3	0	0
Jacob Huber	3	0	0
Sebastian Graff	3	0	0
George Graff	3	0	0
	£54	0	0

This school (57:93) was opened the 1st of July, 1755, with Reverend Samuel Magaw as master. The trustees granted him the privilege to teach Latin and Greek to the children of those who had subscribed. In addition to the regular salary, he was allowed £25 to employ an assistant.

Rev. Schlatter opened the school in New Providence on February 16th, 1755. Charles Cornelius Rabatan was chosen master at £25 per annum, and his wife received £10 to teach eighteen poor children reading and sewing. On the 5th of March, of the same year, Schlatter opened a school in Reading. Conrad Weiser, in behalf of the society, opened schools in Heidelberg and Tulpehocken, April 1st, 1755. John Davies, from Ireland, was selected to teach the schools at £30 per annum. The school in Easton was opened May 16th, with John Middleton master, at an annual salary of £30.

In August, 1755, Mr. Sampson Smith (33:218), the moderator of the Pennsylvania Presbytery, opened a school at Chesnut Level, under the direction of the Trustees-general. Francis Alison (33:227), who subsequently became Professor of Moral Philosophy in the Academy of Philadelphia, was chosen master, at an annual salary of £20, and his assistant was granted £15 per annum. Messrs. Boyd and McDowell, Moses Irwin, James Marshal, Martin Beam and Jacob Graft were appointed deputy trustees, and were instructed to "visit the school every quarter, the third Tuesday, commencing with the third Tuesday of August" (33:174).

The letter of the Trustees-general, dated September 24th, 1756, to the London Society, shows that the early success of these schools was equal to their expectations. The trustees say (57:140), "Upon the whole, they are in as promising a State as can reasonably be expected in a country so much harassed by a Savage Enemy, and subject to so many alarms to disturb that Peace and Tranquillity which are so essentially necessary to the Cultivation of Knowledge. You are already informed that three of the schools We had planted have for some time past been entirely broken up, being near the Frontiers, where the People for near a year have been flying from Place to Place, and but little fixed in their Habitations." Taking into consideration the unsettled condition of the Province at this time, the attendance of these schools speaks well for the earnestness in which these early settlers strove to educate their children. The report of the Society for 1759 gives the total enrollment (15:452):

"Place.	Number of Scholars (Boys).
1. At New Providence, Philadelphia Co., almost all Germans	50
2. At Upper Dublin, Philadelphia Co., one-third Germans...	48
3. At Northampton, Bucks Co., all Low Dutch.............	60
4. At Lancaster, Lancaster Co., nearly one-half Germans...	65
5. At York, York Co., more than one-half Germans.........	66
6. At New Hanover, Berks Co., all Germans................	45
7. At Reading, Berks Co., more than one-half Germans.....	36
8. Chestnut Level, Lancaster Co., Presbytery school for educating the youth for the ministry...................	25
Total	440

N. B.—These numbers were taken just after the harvest, when the schools were but thin. In winter the numbers educated in this Charity often amount in all to nearly 600, and have amounted to 750, before the schools at Easton and Codorus were broken up by the Indian incursions.* Upwards of two-thirds are of German parentage."

The section of the State in which these schools were established embraced almost the entire territory in which German settlements were to be found. Dr. Smith took a deep interest in the movement, and counted it an honor to be its responsible head. On the 12th of March, 1759, the University of Oxford conferred upon him the degree of Doctor of Divinity (57:199). One of the recommendations given by the authorities for bestowing the honor was, "That the said William Smith is also a Trustee for the Free Schools, lately erected, among the vast Body of his Majesty's German Subjects on the Frontiers of Pennsylvania, and Colonies adjacent, by an honorable Society in London; in order to instruct the Children of the said Germans, in the English Tongue and Principles of Protestantism, and defeat the wicked Designs of the French and Papish Emissaries that swarm among them; to which pious Work his sacred Majesty has been a generous and constant Benefactor.

* The report makes no mention of the school at Tulpehocken which was broken up in a similar manner.

"That in Consequence of this Trust, the said William Smith has, besides the Youth of the College, upwards of 700 children continually under his care, in different parts of the Country; that he visits them frequently in their several schools, pays the Master's salaries, and superintends the Execution of the whole Design." During the first two years the schools were visited regularly by Superintendent Schlatter and Dr. Smith. Some of the other members of the Trustees-general paid them occasional visits on their journeys to the frontiers (57:140). In March, 1757, Schlatter, who had resigned his commission as Superintendent the latter part of 1756, was appointed one of the chaplains of the Royal American regiment on military duty in Nova Scotia (65:18). He having resigned as Superintendent of the Charity Schools, the entire care of these schools was left to Dr. Smith and his associates.

While the efforts of the London Society were directed primarily to the maintenance of schools, aid was also given to Lutheran and Calvinist ministers who gave religious and secular instruction to the children of the German Colonists (57:94). The receipts of Dr. Smith, for the year 1755, show that Messrs. Weiss, Heiner and Schlatter, among the Reformed ministers, and Messrs. Handschuh and Muhlenberg, among the Lutheran ministers, received aid from the Society. The Minutes of the Coetus (34:143) of the Reformed churches in Pennsylvania prove conclusively that some of the ministers of the different Reformed congregations received annual sums of money from the Society, though quite irregularly toward the close of the Charity School movement (34:198). The Minutes of the Coetus, of June 17th, 1756, show that the following individual amounts were received from the London Society:

Reverend	Rieger	£10
"	Weiss	10
"	Leydich	10
"	Stoy	10
"	Otterbein	10
"	Steiner	10
"	DuBois	10
"	Lischy	10
"	Waldschmidt	8
"	Tempelman	3
		£91

This was the first donation the Coetus received in this manner, but that the Society continued to distribute money among ministers, as well as schoolmasters, is evident from the following report of the Society for the year 1758, dated January 25th, 1759 (65:17):

1. To the salaries of schoolmasters and assistants, excessive of what is paid by the people......£284 0 0
2. Gratuities to six Lutheran ministers, who are employed as catechists....................... 53 0 0
3. Gratuities to twelve Calvinist ministers.......... 107 0 0
4. The expense of a printing-office, by which a German paper is carried on and Catechisms and other good books printed................... 120 0 0
5. To the German minister at Santee Forks, Carolina 20 0 0

Total £584 0 0
Or £380 sterling money.

This report is of special value because of the fact that it gives the exact amount expended and the manner in which each item was accounted for.

In addition to the foregoing activities it is of interest to note that the Presbyterians came to participate in a movement which was intended solely for the benefit of the Germans.

A committee of the Presbyteries (33:173) of Philadelphia, New Castle and Donegall, met November 16th, 1743, and passed a resolution setting forth "the necessity of using speedy endeavors to educate youth for supplying our vacancies." Immediately after that date, the committee opened a school at New London for the purpose stated above. At a meeting of the Presbyteries in Philadelphia, May 25th, 1744, the committee laid the proposition, to open a school, before the general body. The Synod of Philadelphia approved of the design, and took the school under their care. A board of trustees was appointed "to inspect the master's diligence in, and method of, teaching; consider and direct what authors are chiefly to be read in the several branches of learning; to examine the scholars from time to time, as to their proficiency, etc." (33:174.)

To this academy were admitted the children of all persons who pleased to send them "and have them instructed gratis in the languages, philosophy and divinity." The maintenance of the school depended on such annual contributions as were made by the several congregations of

Synod. In May, 1755, when the contributions realized were found to be inadequate to continue the school any longer, the Presbytery (33:218) ordered, "That application be made to the trustees of the German schools to procure a sum of money to encourage our school, engaging to teach some Dutch children the English tongue and three or four boys Latin and Greek, if they offer themselves." Among the reasons offered why this bounty should be were (33:225): 1. That the school had for the past twelve years given free instruction "to all ranks and denominations that pleased to accept of the same;" 2. The encouragement of schools in the country, supplying them with masters, and keeping them under proper supervision, would contribute much toward making this province a seat of learning in this part of the world and would aid greatly "the growth of the College in this city;" 3. "The school has been as free to the Germans as any other nation, and two of the Reformed ministers, born in this country, were educated there;" 4. The mother church in Scotland contributed largely to the common fund at the disposal of the Society for the Propagation of the Gospel; 5. The petitioners have at heart "the interests of religion, virtue and learning."

Messrs. Cross and Alison were instructed to bear the petition to the Trustees-general and await their instructions. The Synod promised that the school would at once be transferred from New London to Chesnut Level, if the trustees should grant their request. In compliance with their promise the transfer was made after the trustees reported favorably on the petition.

The Trustees-general (33:226) met June 14, 1755, at Judge Allen's house in Mount Airy. Messrs. Allen, Peters, Franklin, and Smith were present and took action on the petition of the Synod. The objection was offered by the trustees, "that to grant the petition in favour of an English Synod, might give offence to the Germans, who generally considered this charity as intended solely for their own particular benefit. The trustees were also of opinion that it did not fall directly under the great design for promoting the English tongue among the Germans." These objections were not of sufficient consequence to counterbalance all the reasons urged by the Synod for the granting of financial aid. The trustees voted the Synod twenty-five pounds currency for one year on the following conditions (33:227):

1. "That it shall be under the same common government with the other free schools, and subject to the visitations of the trustees-general or their deputies, appointed on the recommendation of the Synod.

2. "That the master shall teach four Dutch or English gratis, upon the recommendation of the trustees-general, to be prepared for the ministry, and ten poor Dutch children in the English tongue gratis, if so many offer.

3. "That the deputy trustees, together with the master, and any of the clergy, visit the school, at least once a quarter, and send down a statement thereof to be transmitted by the general trustees to the honorable Society."

The Trustees-general notified the London Society of the action they had taken in regard to the petition presented by the Presbyterian Synod of Philadelphia. A letter which Dr. Smith received, September 14, 1757, from Dr. Chandler (33:229), Secretary of the London Society, explained in detail the answer of the Society to the petition:

"November 27, last, upon the petition of the Synod of Pennsylvania, and the recommendation of our trustees, we have agreed to allow thirty pounds sterling per annum, toward the support of the school mentioned to be erected by them, from midsummer before that date. And I have purchased and packed up, among other books, a large number of English Primers and Spelling Books for their use, and that of the German children, which I hope will soon be sent over to you; as soon, at least, as I can get a safe conveyance."

That the Synod continued to receive aid from the London Society is evident from the minutes of the Presbytery, dated May 20, 1762. Doctor Alison (33:315) informed the Synod that he still had some money left out of the German fund for supporting the school, but that "the fund for the German emigrants is now exhausted, and it is supposed that any other supplies from the fund can hardly be expected." This appears to be the last statement to be found in the Records of the Presbytery of any financial aid the Presbytery school at Chesnut Level received from the London Society.

CHAPTER IV.

FAILURE AND THE CAUSES OF FAILURE.

After Schlatter had resigned as Superintendent of the schools, the Germans had no direct representation in the management of them. Conrad Weiser was still a member of the Trustees-general, but his duties as Indian Interpreter prevented his giving much time and attention to the education of the Germans. On the other hand, Schlatter (65:18) had encountered so much opposition from the Germans on account of the attacks of Saur upon him through the medium of editorials which appeared in the latter's influential newspaper and by private letters addressed by Saur to his friends that he resigned his commission the latter part of 1756.*

On account of the liberal policy of its founder, Pennsylvania was made up of more diverse nationalities than any other colony. Every creed and nationality found here the same welcome. In Philadelphia and the surrounding counties—Philadelphia, Chester and Bucks, the Quakers settled. Encircling this section, were the Germans who occupied the extreme limits of the counties named, and large sections of Lancaster, Berks and Northampton counties. The Scotch-Irish Presbyterians pushed their settlements to the frontiers west of these. Among the English was a small element belonging to the Church of England. Among the German settlers, the Mennonites, Moravians, Dunkers, Schwenkfelders, and the remainder of those Quietist Sects, held to religious principles which were much the same as those of the Quakers. They regarded it unlawful to bear arms or take oaths. In consequence, these Germans formed political affiliations with the Quakers. Christopher Saur was identified with the Dunkers, and used his press as a means to keep the Quakers dominant in the state assembly. This guaranteed a continuation of the peace policy adopted by Penn and his successors. On the other hand, the leaders among the Scotch-Irish Presbyterians, the Church of England, and those Germans who belonged to the Lutheran and Re-

---

*See p. 48.

formed faiths, were not opposed to war. These groups advocated the establishment of state military defenses. In opposition to the peaceful policy which the Quakers stood for in administering the affairs of state, they became known as the war-party.

Saur saw in the Charity School movement a project to array the forces of organized religion against those groups of sects that had no formal ecclesiastical organization. He further regarded it as an attempt to promote the interests of the war-party in the state. This appears in a letter* to a "Dear Friend," dated September 16, 1755 (48), in which he says, "I have received your welcome letter and have answered the same by the bearer. Since then it has occurred to me whether it could really be true that Gilbert Tennent, Schlatter, Peters, Hamilton, Allen, Turner, Schippen, Schmitt (Smith), Franklin, Muhlenberg, Brunnholtz, Handschuh, etc., have the slightest concern for the ignorant Germans in Pennsylvania with a view of their real conversion, or whether the institution of free schools is not rather the means to bring the country into a feeling of turmoil and unrest, etc. Since each one of them has his own grand proposition and private gain involved, and seeks what concerns Hamilton, Peters, Allen, Turner, Schippen and friends, therefore, I know that they concern themselves little about religion and the culture of the minds of the Germans, but that (the Germans) shall offer their services in the militia and defend their property for them. Such people do not know what it is to believe and trust in God. Their riches is their God. Their mortification is complete when they are unable to compel the people to protect their gods. ᶠTennent may well firmly believe that his religion is the best, and if, with Schlatter's aid, it can be brought about that English ministers are provided on a salary for the Germans and that one appoints such ministers in Philadelphia, presses into service and sets apart such God-fearing men in New Jersey, then will Tennent have honor: Schlatter, sustenance. The Germans, to the satisfaction of their benefactors, will elect, without fail, Hamilton, Peters, Schippen, Allen, Turner, &c., &c., to the assembly. These may make a law with R. H. M.† for the construction of a military fortress, its equipment with soldiers, * * * * *, or fix the salaries for ministers and teachers

---

* Original in possession of Dr. M. G. Brumbaugh.
† Governor Robert Hunter Morris.

so that in the future it is no longer necessary to write letters of appeal to Halle giving reports of battles, of which letters they must hereafter be ashamed here, and they will be looked upon as liars when their letters are sent back to them in print. Fiat: Thus we get all of ours back and to this purpose there is no better pretense than the poor Germans."

The suspicions thus aroused among the Germans, that selfish motives actuated the promoters of the Charity School movement, were sufficient to alienate not only those of them who were opposed to war on account of their religious tenets, but also many others who frowned upon any form of duplicity the practice of which would affect them in any way. It was undoubtedly with the purpose in view of winning back the element that had been alienated in this manner that Conrad Weiser and Christopher Saur, Jr., attempted, in 1759, to induce Reverend J. J. Zubly, of South Carolina, to accept the superintendency of the schools. Zubly was, in all probability, the most eminent Reformed preacher in America (13:202). He did not belong to any particular synod. He had the good will of all the Germans. The elder and the younger Saur held him in high esteem (48). They regarded him as a man who was always guided by the purest motives. In a letter* of Dr. Zubly's to Christopher Saur, Jr., dated August, 1759 (49), it is evident that Zubly had been asked to consider the acceptance of directing these educational activities among the Pennsylvania Germans. Subsequent to the receipt of Zubly's letter Saur wrote to Conrad Weiser and enclosed the postscript of Zubly's letter in which Zubly says, "If you do not receive a further reply soon you may tell Mr. Weiser, meanwhile, that if the Trustees desire that I should, by God's will, undertake a visit to you, then everything needful of discussion can be presented at my arrival.

"In order that my congregation and friends may not think that I desire only to wander back and forth under a false pretense, let the Trustees inform me through their Secretary that they think I could be of service to them in furthering their design (if they really think so)." Saur, at the close of his letter to Weiser supplements Zubly's postscript as follows: "Such have I desired to impart to you in case the question came up for consideration in its

---

* Original in possession of Dr. M. G. Brumbaugh.

appropriate place in Philadelphia; and if they (the trustees) should decide to write to him that it might be so arranged that his congregation and friends may see that he does not of his own choice journey back and forth." The subsequent history of the "scheme" to educate the Germans does not show that the Trustees-general took any action upon the proposition of Weiser and Saur. If the proposition had been carried out, the Society would have been strengthened in its efforts by the powerful influence of Saur and his press. Thus the success of the movement would, in all probability, have been assured. Failure to take advantage of this opportunity to reconcile the two forces which were both striving to accomplish the same end, namely, the education of the Germans, resulted in a further disintegration of effort.

The Minutes of the Coetus (34:198) of the Reformed Church, dated June 25th, 1761, show that the schools established by the Society were fast passing out of existence. The report of the Coetus to the Synod in Holland states that "Regarding the free schools, we can hardly say anything, because the entire matter has been taken out of our hands. In general we can say that there are still three schools of which we know; two of them are all English and one half-German." With the year 1763 the support of the King ceased. Secular as well as religious instruction fell wholly into the care of the church.

The history of the close of the Charity School movement is closely identified with the history of the University of Pennsylvania. This is due to the fact that, with the exception of Conrad Weiser, all the members of the Trustees-general who were in charge of the movement, were connected with "The College and Academy of the City of Philadelphia." Dr. Smith was the Provost; Hamilton, Allen, Franklin and Peters were trustees of that institution.

The last reference to the free schools in Pennsylvania, and the manner in which the funds realized from outstanding debts were applied, appear in the old records of the University. Among the Minutes of the Trustees (25:258f), dated April 12th, 1764, is to be found a letter written by Dr. Samuel Chandler to Reverend Peters, in which he says, "As the Schools, etc., are now at End, though I could have obtained his Majestie's Bounty, for ye Continuance of them, had it been of any Consequence to have upheld them longer. You Sr and ye Rest of the Worthy

Trustees have my most warm and sincere thanks for ye Care and Integrity you have shown in this Affair, and I will take Care you have ye Acknowledgment of the Society upon their first Meeting. Your last Account I have received, against which there can be no possible Exception. We have yet some Money left, which I shall use my Endeavors shall be for the most part applied to the Use of the College. You will do extremely well to appropriate whatever outstanding Debts may Come into the Use of ye Charity Schools, for which Purpose I intend to keep in my hands a small sum, that yet remains with me, for which I shall desire at a proper Time to be drawn on." The trustees of the College acknowledged the receipt of Dr. Chandler's letter, June 14th, 1764, and thanked him for his "Kindness in allowing the Residue of the Fund for the German Schools in this Province, to be applied to the Use of the Charity School belonging to this Institution, and acquainting us in your Letter to our President, the Revd. Mr. Peters that you have some Money of this Fund left in your Hands for which you will desire us to draw at a proper time" (25:266).

The meeting of the Trustees of the College held December 19th, 1769 (26:13), Messrs. Laurence, Chew, Peters and Duche being present, resulted in further action being taken as to the disposition of the funds realized from the management of the German schools. The item in the Minutes of the Trustees which refers to the matter in question bears the following import: "In Pursuance of a Letter from Rev. Dr. Chandler, late of the Old Jewry London, to Reverend Mr. Peters, dated London April 20, 1763, & produced to the Board, ordering the Residue of the Money that might be in Mr. Peters Hands after settling all accounts relative to the German Schools, to be paid to the Trustees of the College for the Use of the Charity School; Mr. Peters now reported on the Settlement of his Accounts there remained in his Hands the Sum of Eighty-Eight Pounds, Twelve shillings and four Pence, which he was ready to pay to the Trustees.

"Mr. Peters & Dr. Smith, further informed the Trustees, that Dr. Chandler & the other Trustees for the German Schools in England, had likewise ordered all the monies that might arise on the outstanding Debts, due for German News-Papers, Almanacs, Catechisms, & other Profits from the German Press not yet settled, to be applied towards the Use of the Charity School, as far as they could be collected; and that a large sum remained due, which Messrs. Weiss & Miller* had engaged to collect, but it was believed had neglected it.

"The Trustees request that Mr. Hamilton, Mr. Allen, Mr. Peters and Dr. Smith, who formerly had the Management of the German Charity, would get these Accounts settled with Messrs. Weiss & Miller & the outstanding debts collected and report accordingly to the Trustees as soon as possible."

The "Day-Book" of the Academy of Philadelphia (1:94), under date of May 16th, 1770, shows that the money which Reverend Peters had in his possession was paid to the Academy as had been agreed upon. The item is as follows:

To Account of Subscriptions of Mr. Peters—the
    Balance of his Account with the Society for
    erecting German Schools in the Province of
    Pennsylvania £88 12s 4d

The records kept in the University Archives contain no further reference to any sum or sums of money which were expected to be realized from the products of the printing-press and the other profits spoken of. There are no available sources to show conclusively that any additional amounts were ever collected or, if collected, turned into the University treasury for the use of the Charity School connected with the institution; although such was the evident purpose of the Trustees.

The sudden collapse of this movement was remarkable. Here was a movement of far-reaching consequences had it rested on sound bases. One must be impressed with the general conception of this system of education. There were two responsible bodies which controlled its management: one in England and one in America. To insure closer supervision the responsible board of managers in Pennsylvania was assisted by local deputy-trustees and a personal representative known as the Superintendent. The qualifications of teachers was of a high standard—a fact all the more singular because of the early period in which the system was inaugurated. The courses of study and the manner in which schools were established were exceedingly liberal. Taking it all through, in no other colony had such a perfectly wrought out system of education

---

*See p. 39.

been projected. It must be evident to everyone who studies the system that the cause of its failure did not lie in the system *per se* but that other causes must have worked its downfall.

Beginning with the year 1760 (34:193), the donations of the London Society became so irregular that the support of the schools depended almost entirely on the poor Germans of the communities in which the schools were established. Most of these Germans (34:203) had large families and those who were poor or in moderate circumstances could not afford to devote much money to educational purposes. The well-to-do were comparatively few. This was due in large measure to the fact that large groups of poor immigrants were annually arriving from Germany. The first problem the German had to face was how he might, to the best advantage, clear a few acres of ground and earn a livelihood. The education of his children was of minor importance so long as the home was not secure. The opposition, due to less important considerations, which this plan of education met is summed up in Saur's letter, previously referred to, in which he says (48):

"I live here, as it were, on the corner and hear many people express their thoughts. One says: 'My conscience troubles me to have my children educated out of the funds of the poor, because I do not need it and am able to pay for it.' Others say that where so many children assemble there the child learns from the other something bad before it learns the good. I'll teach my own children reading and writing, and am sorry that others visit them. Others say: 'If the German children learn to speak English and associate with others, then, they will wish to be dressed after the English fashion. One has great difficulty to remove from their minds these foolish notions.' Others say: 'Poor people have no advantage from the benevolence of the King and the Society, if they do not build a school-house every ten miles and keep a teacher. For if a child is obliged to go to, and return from, a school more than five miles distant, it is too far to go there in the morning and return again in the evening. Poor people are not able to let their children be boarded, nor can they clothe them properly to go to school with those of high rank, so that this privilege belongs only to the rich and to the English. The people are to petition to their temporal and eternal ruin.'" No doubt all of the objections offered in Saur's letter were valid reasons for some of the Germans to remain indifferent to the Charity School movement, but the vital opposition the "scheme" encountered was due to the fact that back of it all lurked motives, the carrying out of which, involved the language as well as the political and religious interests of the Germans. It has already been stated that the managers of the movement did not take Saur into their confidence, but, on the contrary, set up a press in opposition to him. Saur, however, with keen-sighted vision, dissected the system of education projected by the Society and exposed to his countrymen, by means of his newspaper and private letters to influential friends, the real motives for its establishment. Although this new press was avowedly the champion of the Society's educational propaganda, it is a fact that within the two and one-half years in which the "Philadelphische Zeitung" was printed not one editorial, in the copies of this paper available, appeared in defense of the Charity School movement.

Dr. Smith, as has already been pointed out, submitted the "scheme" of education to the Society in London. That same scheme formulated by him in greater detail in the "Brief History of the Rise and Progress of the Charitable Scheme, &c.," was adopted by the Trustees-general. It will be remembered that one of the qualifications set forth in that Brief was that "The Youth will be instructed in both the English and German languages."* How this item was carried out may be evinced by an item in the Minutes of the Reformed Coetus (34:157), dated August 24, 1757: "Now with regard to the schools, we can do but little to promote them, since the Directors try to erect nothing but English schools, and care nothing for the German language. Hence, now as before, the Germans themselves ought to look out for their schools, in which their children may be instructed in German." This actual state of affairs was in complete harmony with "the great design for promoting the English tongue among the Germans."† Here was a patent attempt to take away from the Germans their language—a treasure which they guarded as jealously as their religious rights. They were far from being "totally ignorant." Such an insinuation seems wholly unwarranted when the facts in the case show that the great majority of them could read and write. Although most

*See p. 41.
†See p. 50.

of them had only a fair amount of intelligence, the scholar was not absent in their number. Such men as Pastorius, Rittenhouse, Schlatter, Muhlenberg, Weiser, Peter Miller, Saur, Dock, and Zinzendorf bear comparison with an equal number of scholars among other nationalities in Colonial Pennsylvania. The statement that the German immigrants were "the most stupid of their nation" scarcely bears investigation when it is remembered that printing-presses flourished among them, that newspapers, almanacs and books abounded in the majority of German homes.

It is a safe inference that the children of the German immigrants, on account of the lack of opportunity in many instances to get an education, were intellectually inferior to their parents, but the various denominations made provision for these as fast as the German settlements in any community were sufficiently numerous to establish schools and churches. Where this was impossible ignorance was inevitable. These people saw in the Charity School project a scheme to rob them of their language and literature. This caused them to oppose it.

It is evident that there was ample need for such a "scheme" as that of the Charity Schools, but its operation brought the movement under suspicion and open opposition because of its perverted aims. The repression of the German language was but the initial step to inculcate political principles. The Germans who had hitherto opposed war, either on religious grounds or on the assumption that an anti-war standard was synonymous with a no-tax standard, were chary of any movement of the Trustees-general, nearly all of whom were among the leaders of the political party which favored a strong military defense of the frontiers. The statement that there was a widespread danger that the Germans were on the verge of joining the French Catholics to expel the English, can only be regarded as a means to raise funds to establish a movement one of whose ulterior purposes was to fortify the war-party against the Quakers and those Germans who voted with the Quakers. That there can be no question that such political purposes were uppermost in the minds of the trustees is evinced by the fact that the printing-press established by them was used for printing (55:48f) "Rules and Articles of War." The Germans, by means of Saur's warnings and their own practical foresight, detected the trend of affairs and, for the most part, refused to have anything further to do with the Charity Schools.

The efforts of Messrs. Smith and Peters to promote by means of this educational system the interests of the Church of England constituted another factor which contributed largely to the early abandonment of the entire plan. It inevitably led to a lack of patronage. This motive appears again and again in the correspondence of these men. A few examples will serve to justify this statement.

In a letter which Dr. Smith (57:145) wrote to the Bishop of Oxford, November 1st, 1756, he speaks of the need of establishing missions on the frontiers to prevent the "disaffected Germans" from joining with the "French-German" colony settled in the State. Continuing, he says, "It was from the same apprehension I so warmly pressed, and so earnestly engaged in, the scheme for planting English schools among our Germans, which now flourish as well as the distracted state of the Country permits; and Your Lordship may depend, that they shall always be conducted with 'a due regard to the interests of the Church of England.' For, in truth, it is but one part of the same noble scheme in which the venerable Society are engaged; and wherever there are missionaries near any of the schools, they are either employed as Masters, or named among the deputy trustees and Managers of the school. In short, till we can succeed in making our Germans speak English and become good Protestants, I doubt we shall never have a firm hold on them. For this reason, the extending the means of their instruction, as far as they extend their settlement, is a matter that deserves our most attentive consideration. I am pleased therefore that your Lordship, and the Society, have given me leave to mention such other places on the frontiers as may be fit to place Missionaries in, so that the Kingdom of Christ may keep pace in its growth, with the growth of the English Colonies. This liberty I shall not fail to make due use of, and likewise offer a scheme for uniting with the Church, all the German Lutherans of this Country; which I am sure would easily take effect."

The Church of England in Pennsylvania was weaker in number than most of the other religious denominations; in consequence, those who stood high in the councils of the Church in the Province were anxious to give it a more significant position.

In 1765, Reverend Richard Peters (32:433), the treasurer of the German fund, sent to the Bishop of London a letter of introduction with Dr. Charles Magnus Wrangel, the provost of the Swedish Churches in America from 1759 to 1768, in which he proposes a plan to unite with the Church of England the German Lutherans and the Swedes: "Dr. Wrangel wants to take a just advantage of this general antipathy to the Presbyterians, and to unite the great body of Lutherans and Swedes with the Church of England, who, you know, are but few and in mean circumstances in this province, but, were they united with the German Lutherans, we should both become respectable. This Dr. Smith and I think may be done by the means of our academy. We might have a professorship of divinity opened in it wherein German and English youth might be educated, and by having both languages as a part of their education they might preach both in German and English in such places where there is a mixture of both nations. This would conciliate us all and make us live and love as one nature. It is a happy thought. I wish your lordship would talk with Dr. Wrangel and encourage it all you can."

Reverend Thomas Barton (32:267), another clergyman in Pennsylvania belonging to the Church of England went so far, in 1764, as to suggest compulsory measures to effect a complete incorporation of the Germans with the English Church. In a letter to the Society for the Propagation of Religion in Foreign Parts, he says: "The Germans in general are well affected to the Church of England, and might easily be brought over to it. A law obliging them to give their children an English Education, which could not be deemed an abridgment of their liberty (as British Subjects), would soon have this effect."

Saur was undoubtedly wrong in his charge that Tennent, Schlatter, Peters, Hamilton, Allen, etc., were interested in the movement for merely selfish ends, but he was right in so far as he acquainted the Germans with the real purposes of this educational project. These were the underlying motives which Saur exposed. He influenced the great body of Germans against the scheme which was intended for their education. In his opinions the general sentiment of the Germans was crystallized. No doubt Dr. Smith and his associates were sincere in their efforts to educate the Germans. The funds raised and expended for this purpose, the time and energy devoted by the London Society and its agents to make the "scheme" a success, were far too great to warrant any other conclusion. But it is evident that the motives set forth that the "Charitable Scheme" was intended to better the intellectual and moral conditions were alloyed with political and ecclesiastical aspirations. On the other hand, Saur and the German constituency which he represented through the medium of his press, resented what was not open and above board. They were not opposed to the English language, nor to education, nor to the Royal and the Provincial governments. They loved their language. They were eager to obtain a common school education sufficient to pursue their occupation successfully. Though there was an undesirable element among them, the great majority of them were respectable citizens of the Commonwealth. There were many religious denominations among them, and each denomination held tenaciously to its own creed. To represent them in any other light than what has just been stated, to attempt to force them blindly into a political allegiance the equity of which they had not been led to see, to interfere with their religious tenets;—meant open opposition. This was the fate of the Charity School movement. Whether the Germans were right, under the circumstances, in the position they took on this question depends upon one's point of view. Construed in the light of national pride, integrity of language and religion, they pursued a natural course. But by standing aloof from a system which, if properly carried on, would have meant a more rapid unity among the different political elements in the state as well as greater opportunities for the Germans to rise in intellectual and political influence, they took a wrong step.

Yet, the system was not without its good effects. It stimulated the Germans to maintain the integrity of their language and religion, to provide churches and schools for that purpose, to disprove the false charges affecting their loyalty to the government by the heroic part taken by them in the Revolutionary War. It also broke the ground for the establishment of public schools by legislative enactment in 1834.

The bearing of these Germans throughout this long, and to them vital contest, is ample vindication of the wisdom of William Penn in inviting them into his province. True to the principles they had set up as standards, walking in the light as they saw it, open to conviction but

averse to any form of coercion, they added strength to
the state, honor to the nation.

This is the greatest educational struggle in Colonial
America. While divers creeds and nationalities of other
colonies struggled to settle their differences with sword
and bayonet, Pennsylvania true to the spirit of its founder
unified her people, differing in nationality, religion and
industrial pursuits, with the implements of peace,—the
school, the church and the press.

BIBLIOGRAPHY.

1. ACADEMY OF PHILADELPHIA.
   Day-Book (Dec., 1749-May, 1789). University Archives. No. 40. 94. [57.]

2. ACRELIUS, ISRAEL.
   A History of New Sweden; The Settlement on the River Delaware. Translated from the Swedish by William M. Reynolds, D.D. Philadelphia: Publication Fund of the Historical Society of Pennsylvania, 1874. 351, 352. [22.]

3. AMERICAN BROADSIDES (1708-1772).
   H. 1292. The Historical Society of Pennsylvania. (London, about 1754.) 66. [26.]

4. ANNALS OF THE GENERAL ASSEMBLY OF THE CHURCH OF SCOTLAND, from the Final Secession in 1739 to the Origin of the Relief in 1752: With an Appendix of Biographical Sketches, Illustrative Documents and Notes. Edinburgh: John Johnstone, 1838. 293, 294. [25.]

5. ANNALS OF THE GENERAL ASSEMBLY OF THE CHURCH OF SCOTLAND, from the Origin of the Relief of 1752 to the Rejection of the Overture on Schism in 1766: With an Appendix of Biographical Sketches, Illustrative Documents and Notes. Edinburgh: John Johnstone, 1840. 25, 26. [25, 26.]

6. BRIGGS, CHARLES AUGUSTUS, D. D.
   American Presbyterianism: Its Origin and Early History. Together with an Appendix of Letters and Documents, many of which have recently been discovered. New York: Chas. Scribner's Sons, 1885. (Appendix—104, 106, 107.) 312. [24, 25.]

7. BRUMBAUGH, MARTIN GROVE.
A History of the German Baptist Brethren in Europe and America. Brethren Publishing House, Mount Morris, Illinois, 1899. 345. [35.]

8. CASSEL, DANIEL K.
History of the Mennonites. Philadelphia: Daniel K. Cassel, 1888. 182. [15.]

9. COBB, SANFORD H.
The Story of the Palatines—An Episode in Colonial History. New York and London: G. P. Putnam & Sons. The Knickerbocker Press, 1897. 282. [9.]

10. DIFFENDERFFER, FRANK RIED.
The German Immigration into Pennsylvania through the Port of Philadelphia from 1700-1775. Part II. The Redemptioners. Lancaster, Pa. Pa. German Society. Vol. X, No. 2. 1900. 10-11, 102, 105f, 118. [9, 10.]

11. DOCK, CHRISTOPH.
Eine Einfältige und gründlich abgefaszte Schul-Ordnung, Darinnen deutlich vorgestellt wird, auf welche Weisze die kinder nicht nur in denen in Schulen gewähnlichen Lehren bestens angebracht, sondern auch in der Lehre der Gottseligkeit wohl unterrichtet werden mögen. Germantown: Gedruckt und zu finden bey Christoph Saur, 1770. 14, 15, 25. [19, 20.]

12. DOCUMENTARY HISTORY OF THE EVANGELICAL LUTHERAN MINISTERIUM OF PENNSYLVANIA AND ADJACENT STATES. Proceedings of Annual Conventions from 1748 to 1821. Philadelphia: Board of Publication of the General Council of the Evangelical Lutheran Church of North America, 1898. 10. [16.]

13. DUBBS, JOSEPH HENRY, D.D., LL.D.
The Reformed Church in Pennsylvania. Part IX of a Narrative and Critical History Prepared at the Request of the Pennsylvania-German Society. Lancaster, Pa., 1092. 160, 202. [15, 54.]

14. ETLICHE CHRISTLICHE GEBATE.

Welche Die versammlte Glaubigen, oder ein jeder absonderlich nach Gelegenheit der zeit und der Sachen Nothwendigkeit (für Gott) mit Andact und gebeugten knien der Herzens gebrauchen mögen. Germantown: Gedruckt bei Michael Billmeyer, 1790. 223. [20.]

15. GOOD, JAMES I., REV. PROF.

History of the Reformed Church in the United States (1725-1792). Reading, Pa.: Daniel Miller, Publisher, 1899. 452. [47.]

16. HARBAUGH, REV. H.

The Life of Reverend Michael Schlatter, with a Full Account of his Travels and Labors among the Germans. Philadelphia: Lindsay & Blakiston, 1857. 198, 203-205, 208, 213, 236, 248. [21, 23, 24.]

17. JACOBS, HENRY EYSTER.

A History of the Evangelical Lutheran Church in the United States. Second Edition. New York: Charles Scribner's Sons, 1899. 279. [33.]

18. JACOBS, HENRY EYSTER.

The German Emigration to America (1709-1740). Part III of A Narrative and Critical History, prepared at the Request of "The Pennsylvania-German Society." Lancaster, Pa., 1898. 137, 138. [8.]

19.. KELKER, L. N.

Division of Public Records. Pennsylvania State Library, Harrisburg, Pa. [14.]

20. KRIEBEL, HOWARD WIEGNER.

The Schwenkfelders in Pennsylvania. Lancaster, Pa., 1904. 35. [8.]

21. KUHNS, OSCAR.

The German and Swiss Settlements of Colonial Pennsylvania: A Study of the So-called Pennsylvania Dutch. New York: Henry Holt & Co., 1901. 55. [9.]

22. MANN, W. J.; SMUCKER, B. M.; GERMANN, W.
Nachrichten von den vereinigten Deutschen
Evangelisch-Lutherischen Gemeinen in Nord-
America, absonderlich in Pennsylvania. Halle,
1787. Allentown, Pa., Brobst, Diehl & Co.,
1886.
a. Erster Band: 14, 16, 24, 73, 88, 418, 432,
483, 485. [10, 15, 16, 21, 22.]
b. Zweiter Band: 57, 208. [24, 30.]

23. McMASTER, JOHN BACH.
A History of the People of the United States,
from the Revolution to the Civil War. Vol. II.
New York: D. Appleton & Company, 1885.
557. [10, 11.]

24. MITTELBERGER, GOTTLIEB.
Journey to Pennsylvania in the Year 1750, and
Return to Germany in 1754, etc. Translated
from the German by Carl Theodore Eben.
Philadelphia: John Jos. McVey, 1898. 59, 60,
61, 62. [14, 21.]

25. MINUTES OF THE COLLEGE AND ACADEMY OF PHILA-
DELPHIA. No. I. (1749-1768.) 258, 259, 266.
[55, 56.]

26. MINUTES OF THE COLLEGE AND ACADEMY OF THE CITY
OF PHILADELPHIA. (1768-1791.) University Archives. 13. [56, 57.]

27. MURPHY, THOMAS, D.D.
The Presbytery of The Log College; or, The
Cradle of the Presbyterian Church in America.
Philadelphia: Presbyterian Board of Publica-
tion and Sabbath-school Work. 1889. 66ff.
[28.]

28. PENN, WILLIAM.
Frame of Government of 1682, and Privileges
and Concessions of 1701. Liberty Bell Leaflets. Translations and Reprints from Original
Historical Documents. No. 3. Edited by
Brumbaugh & Walton. Philadelphia: Christopher Sower Co., 1898. 6. [15.]

29. PENNSYLVANIA ARCHIVES—SECOND SERIES.
Printed under direction of William Francis Har-
rity, Secretary of the Commonwealth. Edited by
William H. Egle, M.D. Vol. XVII. Harrisburg: E. K. Meyers, State Printer, 1890. 7-451.
[9.]

30. PENNSYLVANIA ARCHIVES—SECOND SERIES.
Published under direction of Matthew S. Quay,
Secretary of Commonwealth. Edited by John B.
Linn and William H. Egle, M.D. Vol. II. Har-
risburg: B. F. Meyers, State Printer, 1876. 347,
686ff. [12, 13.]

31. PENNYPACKER, SAMUEL W.
Historical and Biographical Sketches. Philadelphia, Pa.: Robert A. Tripple, 1883. 29, 30, 31,
91-95. [8, 19.]

32. PERRY, WILLIAM STEVENS, D.D.
Historical Collection Relating to the American
Colonial Church. Vol. II. Pennsylvania, 1871.
256f, 367, 433. [12, 13, 62.]

33. RECORDS OF THE PRESBYTERIAN CHURCH IN THE
UNITED STATES OF AMERICA, embracing the Min-
utes of the Presbyteries of Philadelphia and New
York (1706-1788). Philadelphia: Presbyterian
Board of Publication, 1841. 173, 174, 218, 225,
226, 227, 229, 315. [49, 50, 51.]

34. REFORMED CHURCH PUBLICATION BOARD.
Minutes and Letters of the Coetus of the German
Reformed Congregation in Pennsylvania (1747-
1792). Together with Three Preliminary Reports of Rev. Jno. P. Boehm (1734-1744). Philadelphia: Reformed Church Publication Board,
1903. 143, 157, 193, 198, 203. [55, 58, 59.]

35. REICHEL, REV. LEVIN THEODORE.
The Early History of the United Brethren, commonly called Moravians, in North America
(1734-1748). Nazareth, Pa.: The Moravian
Historical Society, 1888. 81, 201ff. [8, 21.]

56469

36. RUPP, I. DANIEL.
A Collection of Upwards of Thirty Thousand
Names of German, Swiss, Dutch and Other Immigrants in Pennsylvania, from 1727 to 1776.
Second revised and enlarged edition. Philadelphia: Leary, Stuart & Co., 1898. 49-152, 49-
419. [9.]

37. RUPP, I. DANIEL.
History of Lancaster and York Counties. Lancaster, Pa.: Gilbert Hills, 1845. 294, 440, 441.
[16, 19.]

38. RUPP, I. DANIEL.
History of Northampton, Lehigh, Monroe, Carbon
and Schuylkill Counties. Harrisburg, Pa.:
Hickok & Cantine, Printers and Binders, 1845.
7. [15.]

39. SAUR, CHRISTOPHER, SR.
Biblia, Das ist: Die Heilige Schrift Altes und
Neues Testaments, Nach der Deutschen Uebersetzung D. Martin Luthers, Mit jedes Capitels
kurtzen Summarien, auch beigefügten vielen
und richtigen Parallelen: Nebst einem Anhang
Des dritten und vierten Buchs Esra und dritten
Buchs der Maccabäes. Germantown: Gedruckt
bei Christoph Saur, 1743. 1. [36.]

40. SAUR, CHRISTOPHER, SR.
Pensylvanische Berichte, oder Sammlung, Wich-
tiger Nachrichten aus dem Natur und Kirchen-
Reich. Germantown: Gedruckt und zu finden
bei Chr. Saur, March 1, 1749. 2. [10, 11.]

41. SAUR, CHRISTOPHER, SR.
Der Hoch-Deutsch Amerikanische Kalender.
1752. Germantown: Gedruckt und zu finden
bei Christoph Saur. 24, 25. [17, 18, 19.]

42. SAUR, CHRISTOPHER, SR.
Pensylvanische Berichte, etc. November 1st,
1753. 3, Col. I. [35.]

43. SAUR, CHRISTOPHER, SR.
Der Hoch-Deutsch Amerikanische Kalender,
1754. 24. [37.]

44. SAUR, CHRISTOPHER, SR.
Pensylvanische Berichte, etc. Vor den 1sten September, 1754. 2, 3. [38, 39.]

45. SAUR, CHRISTOPHER, SR
Der Hoch-Deutsch Amerikanische Kalender, 1755. 24. [35.]

46. SAUR, CHRISTOPHER, SR.
Letter to Governor Denny, of Pennsylvania, dated May 12, 1755, Germantown Pa. [10.]

47. SAUR, CHRISTOPHER, SR.
Letter to Governor Denny, of Pennsylvania, dated March 15, 1755, Germantown, Pa. [8.]

48. SAUR, CHRISTOPHER, SR.
Letter to ———, dated September 16, 1755, Germantown, Pa. [53f, 58.]

49. SAUR, CHRISTOPHER, JR.
Letter to Conrad Weiser, dated August, 1759, Germantown, Pa. 54f.

50. SAUR, CHRISTOPHER, JR.
Biblia, Das ist; Die Heilige Schrift Altes und Neues Testaments, Nach der Teutschen Uebersetzung D. Martin Luthers, etc. Germantown: Gedruckt bei Christoph Saur, 1763. 1. [36.]

51. SAUR, CHRISTOPHER, JR.
Ein Geistliches Magazien, Oder: Aus den Schätzen der Schrift gelehrten zum Himelreich gelehrt, Dargereichtes. Altes und Neues. 1764. Vol. I. No. 50, No. 1, A₃. 410. [36, 37.] Vol. II. No. 15. [20.]

52. SCHMAUK, THEODORE EMANUEL.
A History of the Lutheran Church in Pennsylvania. (1638-1820.) Vol. I. Philadelphia: General Council Publishing House, 1903. 233, 234 [8.]

(72)

53. SEIDENSTICKER, OSWALD.
First German Immigration to America. Translation from Bilder aus der Deutsch-Pennsylvanischen Geschichte. University of Pennsylvania Library. 3f, 14, 2, 61, 75. [7, 8, 11.]

54. SEIDENSTICKER, OSWALD.
German-American Events, Principally of Pennsylvania, up to 1870, Collected and Chronologically arranged. 1-4. [8, 12.]

55. SEIDENSTICKER, OSWALD.
The First Century of German Printing in America (1728-1830). Published by the German Pionier-Verein of Philadelphia. Philadelphia: Schaefer & Koradi, 1893. 6-42, 11, 6-100, 45, 48, 52. [21, 36, 37, 39, 60.]

56. SMITH, WM. (ANONYMOUS).
A Brief State of the Province of Pennsylvania. The third edition. London: Printed for R. Griffiths in Pater-noster-Row, 1756. 6, 17f, 28, 29, 31, 34, 37, 38, 41ff. [11, 12, 13, 21, 28.]

57. SMITH, HORACE WEMYSS.
Life and Correspondence of the Rev. William Smith, D.D. Vol. I. Philadelphia: Published by S. A. George & Co., No. 15 N. Seventh St., 1879. 26ff, 29f, 31, 34f, 36, 40f, 42, 45, 48, 64, 65, 66, 69, 70, 71f, 80, 81, 88, 89, 90, 93, 94, 96f, 102, 145f, 197ff, 220. [11, 13, 14, 15, 26, 27, 28, 29, 31, 32, 33, 34, 38, 39, 40, 44, 45, 46, 47, 48, 61.]

58. SOWER, CHAS. G.
Genealogical Chart of the Descendants of Christopher Sower, Printer, of Germantown, Philadelphia, Pa. Philadelphia, 1887. Columns 1 and 2. [37.]

59. SPARKS, JARED.
The Works of Benjamin Franklin; Containing several Political and Historical Tracts not included in any former edition, etc. Vol. VII. Boston: Whittemore, Niles & Hall, 1856. Milwaukee: A. Whittemore & Co. 66, 71, 72. [11, 13, 14, 20.]

60. STAPLETON, REV. A.

Memorials of the Huguenots in America. With
Special Reference to their Emigration to Penn-
sylvania. Carlisle, Pa.: Huguenot Publishing
Co., 1901. 36f. [10.]

61. STOEVER, MARTIN LUTHER.

Memoirs of "The Life and Times of Henry Mel-
chior Muhlenberg, D.D." For the Lutheran
Board of Publication. Philadelphia: Lindsay &
Blakiston, 1856. 35, 59f, 69. [16, 34.]

62. THE COLONIAL RECORDS OF PENNSYLVANIA. Vol. III.
283. [9.]

63. THOMAS, GABRIEL.

Description of Pennsylvania, 1698. Geography
and History of the Province. No. 5, Part 1.
Liberty Bell Leaflets. Translations and Reprints
from Original Historical Documents. Edited by
Brumbaugh and Walton. Philadelphia: Christopher Sower Co., 1900. 9-10. [10.]

64. THOMAS, ISAIAH.

The History of Printing in America. Second edition. Vol. I. Albany, N. Y.: Joel Munsell,
Printer, 1874. 271. [15, 35.]

65. THE PENNSYLVANIA-GERMAN. An Illustrated Quarterly Magazine devoted to the History, Biography,
Genealogy, Poetry, Folk-Lore and General Interests of the Pennsylvania Germans and their
Descendants. Lebanon, Pa.: October, 1900. Vol.
I. No. 4. Rev. P. C. Croll, A.M., Editor. 6,
13, 14, 17, 18. [23, 24, 30, 48, 49, 52.]

66. TRAVIS, REV. WILLIAM.

History of the Germantown Academy: Compiled
from the Minutes of the Trustees, from 1760 to
1877. Edited by Horace Wemyss Smith.
Philadelphia: Ferguson Bros. & Co., 1882.
8, 10, 13. [37.]

67. TRUSTEES-GENERAL, FOR THE MANAGEMENT OF THE
SAID CHARITABLE SCHEME. A Brief History of the
Rise and Progress of the Charitable Scheme
Carrying on by a Society of Noblemen and

Gentlemen in London, For the Relief and Instruction of poor Germans and their Descendents, Settled in Pennsylvania and the Adjacent British Colonies in North America. Philadelphia: B. Franklin and D. Hall, 1755. 4, 5, 7f, 10ff. [24, 25, 30, 40ff.]

68. WICKERSHAM, JAMES PYLE.

A History of Education of Pennsylvania, Private and Public, Elementary and Higher. Lancaster, Pa.: Inquirer Publishing Company, 1886. 43-57, 140f, 315ff. [16, 28, 37.]

69. WILLIAMS, SAMUEL GORDNER.

The History of Modern Education. Second edition, revised and enlarged. Syracuse, N. Y.: C. W. Bardeen, 1896. 28, 29, 30. [7.]

70. WRIGHT, REV. JOHN.

Early Bibles of America. New York: Thomas Whitaker, 1892. 9, 28, 40, 56. [21, 36.]

56469

370.9748
W38

Date Due

DEC. 7 '78			